KU-762-111

WHAT'S IN THE NEWS ?

A selection of newspaper extracts with exercises

Geoffrey Land

Longman

Contents

Introduction

Learning a language is not merely an academic exercise. Students of English want to be able to use the language they have acquired in the same way as English people use it. They not only want to understand spoken English and to make themselves understood; they also want to be able to appreciate English television and radio programmes, to laugh at English jokes, to sing English songs and to read English newspapers. This last wish often gives rise to some disappointment, when, for example, the student who has passed his exams with top marks and has earned the commendation of his teacher finds that he is quite unable to understand the newspapers which he knows English people read every day. He realises that he lacks something.

The deficiency is not entirely his fault. The difficulty lies in the fact that British newspapers have a style all of their own; or – rather – each paper has its own individual style forming part of a general journalistic pattern which we may loosely classify as 'Newspaper English'. The more popular dailies use a chatty, slangy, up-to-the moment way of writing, which, as often as not, leaves the foreign reader very bewildered, if not under a totally false impression. Here is a typical piece of such reporting:

> Curvaceous Patricia Potts, the girl with the smashing silhouette who was Scunthorpe's Dish of the Month in October – the dishiest dish in the area – was dished up with a dish of trouble on her way home from bingo last night. Two would-be muggers tried it on in Dark Street near her home, but she sent them packing with handbag a-whirling, nails a-scratching and platform clogs a-kicking.

Even the most conscientious student might be forgiven for giving up at this point. And yet it must be realised that this style carries no problems for the millions that read it every day.

Headlines are another problem. The English reader scans the headlines to find out what the news stories are about; the foreign student has to read the stories to find out what the headlines mean.

The popular press, in order to print as much information in as small a space as possible, has developed a content-packed sentence, very often crammed with compound words of a highly complicated nature, that needs to be treated warily at first. For example:

> Warwickshire police announced late last night that Arthur Prentice, a 35-year-old lorry driver of Babblesthorpe, Cambridgeshire, wanted in connection with the disappearance of 17-year-old Glenys Dennis from her home in Cambridge last March, had been arrested in the Solihull area of Birmingham and was helping police with their enquiries.

There are at least fifteen facts in this one sentence. Such writing has to be digested very slowly. If the student of English attempts to absorb a lot of this sort of thing at speed, he will find himself suffering from acute mental indigestion – and will understand very little of what he has read.

In choosing the extracts in this book, I have tried to introduce my readers to 'Newspaper English' gradually. If the passages are read very slowly and carefully, students will find that after the first few sections they have grown accustomed to this rather special way of writing, and that 'newspaper language' is not as difficult as it appears at first sight.

Aims

It must not be thought for a moment that this book has any intention of training students to write for newspapers, or even in a newspaper style. The main aim is to teach them how to understand passages that are packed with factual material, and from this point it is quite clear that reading comprehension tests, such as those to be found in the Cambridge examinations, have been kept firmly in mind during the compilation of the book. There are multiple-choice questions to familiarise the student with this examination technique.

Strong emphasis is laid upon vocabulary extension and amplification, and upon constructional difficulties, but always with reference to the material in the newspaper article. Such exercises, I believe, have far more impact if they are seen to be related to something that has already been encountered in reading.

The frequent exercises based upon reducing paragraphs to 'headlines', and the summary question that comes near the end of each section, have been planned in this way because it seems to me the only realistic method of giving training in précis writing – that rather drily academic exercise so beloved of examining bodies. If someone is asked to reduce a certain piece of English from 300 words to 100, it may well seem a meaningless and useless chore with no reference to the living language. On the other hand, if he is asked to put himself in the position of a sub-editor, who has space for only a hundred words at his disposal and has a 300-word story to fit into it, the exercise takes on a new dimension and a new reality.

Teachers who have had to battle with the formidable problems of précis writing will also recognise the questions in which a number of baldly worded facts have been given and the student has to fit them into a compound sentence (for example, question 4 page 13, and question 2 page 41). The facts given are the notes that the student has made after reading the passage to be summarised; the compound sentence is his finished précis.

And the headline is the ne plus ultra of précis writing – the article reduced to five or six words.

The Gambols strip-cartoons may appear to be just fun items but they are, in fact, far more than that. Here I am trying a new approach to another favourite of the language-teaching world – the guided composition. I have long been of the opinion that only visual impulses can make this a realistic exercise, and these cartoons lend themselves to this very well. I have intentionally chosen only the Gambols for this spot in the book, instead of aiming at a more representative selection from the daily press, for two reasons; firstly, because the strip usually has a fairly strong story line and each episode is self-contained, and secondly because familiarity with the two protagonists helps the student to understand the situations more clearly. In addition, the language used is not too remote from that familiar to the intermediate student of the English language. (I realise, however, that this will not go far to preparing the users of this book for an understanding of the linguistic peculiarities of Andy Capp, or Lil' Abner, or Peanuts.)

How to use the book

The exercises following each press cutting are to be used at the teacher's discretion and I would be reluctant to impose any rules. The use of the exercises will depend upon the nature of the classes, or of the individual students, using the book. Obviously, what is suitable for one class is not necessarily suitable for the next, and the teacher must gauge which exercises are to be given special emphasis and which are to be left out. The following suggestions are given for guidance.

1   The cuttings themselves have been graded, as far as this has been possible, according to difficulty, and their respective exercises have been written with this grading in mind. It is, therefore, advisable to follow the book through from section 1 to the end, and not to select sections at random.

2   Every exercise has a direct bearing on the content or the vocabulary of the news item, and so the first essential is a thorough understanding of the passage. It must be read with great care, and no attempt must be made at any of the exercises until the students – and the teacher – are quite satisfied that everything has been understood.

3   The multiple-choice questions, the content/sentence-forming questions, and the vocabulary-extension questions can be set as homework or done in class. But there are many questions which obviously lend themselves to homework rather than to class activity. These come at the end of each section, and may be loosely classed as composition exercises.

4   The teacher must not be afraid to omit any question that he thinks unsuitable for his class. In fact, the number of varied composition exercises pitches the teaching level at a rather

academic point on the scale, perhaps at that of students preparing for the Cambridge and similar examinations. Students not preparing for such examinations could well leave out several of them, because it will be found that none of the exercises is dependent upon a previous one, although each depends upon the text of the news item.

I hope that students will enjoy using this book, and that teachers will find it both useful and entertaining. I would like to point out that every one of these thirty sections has a text that has recently appeared in the press, and they are not items specially concocted for classroom use. Wherever possible, the articles have been reproduced together with any accompanying photographs, as they actually appeared in the newspapers: a few have had to be reset for the sake of greater clarity. However, in using this book the student is virtually reading items from newspapers. The next step, to the newspapers themselves, is a relatively simple and painless one.

G.S.L.

Acknowledgements

We are grateful to the following for permission to reproduce copyright material:

Associated Newspapers Group Limited for the articles 'The First Blackbird' from the *Daily Mail* 26th May, 1973, 'Hospital Collapses' from *Daily Mail* 10th November, 1971, 'Scientist Warns of Armchair Blaze Danger' from *Daily Mail* in December, 1973, 'No School for 50 Motorway Children' from *Daily Mail* 10th May, 1973 and 'Gas Won't Kill Mouse' from *Daily Mail* 19th January, 1972; Associated Press Newsfeatures for the articles 'Italy finally defeats U.K. in Soccer' from *International Herald Tribune* 15th June, 1973, 'New Swiss Guards Enrolled at Vatican Ceremony' from *The Daily American* 8th May, 1973 and 'Blacksmith Laments Absence of Horses' from *The Daily American* 18th January, 1972; Britannia Airways Ltd. for an advertisement 'Britannia Airways' from the *Daily Express* 8th May, 1973; The Canadian Government Office of Tourism for an advertisement 'There's Nothing Small' from *Punch* magazine 14th March, 1973; Inter-Continental Features for the 'Dear Abby' column by Abigail Van Buren from *The Daily American* 24th/25th September, 1972. © by Chicago Tribune–N.Y. News Synd., Inc; Daily Telegraph for articles 'Propeller hits Man' from *Daily Telegraph* 21st May, 1973, 'Jade Stolen in Mayfair' from *Daily Telegraph* 16th June, 1973, 'Chinese Acrobats of Brilliant Charm' from *Daily Telegraph* 5th July, 1973 and 'Six Firemen Die Searching for Colleague' from *Daily Telegraph* 26th August, 1972; East Anglian Daily Times for an article 'Blaze shock for fire officer' from *East Anglian Daily Times* 7th April, 1973; Eastern Counties Newspapers Limited for articles 'Boy, 14 Rescued from Cliff Face' from *Eastern Daily Press* 18th June, 1973, 'Two injured by blast in caravan' from *Eastern Daily Press* 11th April, 1973 and 'Art world mourns Picasso' from *Eastern Daily Press* 9th April, 1973; The Guardian for two articles 'Stolen Car had been buried' from *The Guardian* 5th April, 1973 and 'Doctor's Home Cure' from *The Guardian* 29th September, 1972; The Controller of Her Majesty's Stationery Office for three advertisements 'There aren't many jobs this secure' from *Daily Express* 8th May, 1973, 'Work in a Job Where you are Needed Every Day' from *Daily Express* 8th May, 1973 and 'He's got all the answers' from *Daily Mail* 10th May, 1973 "Crown copyright, reproduced by permission of the Controller of Her Majesty's Stationery Office"; London Express News Features Services for the article 'For Rescuer Randy – a Surprise Ending' by Webster Anderson from *Sunday Express* 6th May, 1973 and the article 'His Heart Stays in San Francisco' by David Wigg from *Daily Express* 26th March, 1973; The New York Times for the article 'The Migrant Life' from the *International Herald Tribune* 19th September, 1972. © 1971 by The New York Times Company. Reprinted by permission; Punch Publications Limited for an article 'Cinema' by Richard Mallett from *Punch* magazine 23rd August, 1972. 'Reproduced by permission of *Punch*'; Syndication International for an article 'Sunk! A QE2' from *Daily Mirror* 29th September, 1972; Times Newspapers Limited for articles '12 British Children injured in Crash' from *The Times* 30th May, 1973 and 'Five Feared Lost After Sinking of Scots Ship' from *The Times* 30th June, 1973. 'Reproduced from The Times by Permission', 'Barbara Cartland, authoress' from The *Sunday Times* and 'The Quick Brown Fox and The Lazy Dog' by George Perry from The *Sunday Times Magazine*.

We regret we have been unable to trace the copyright holders of the following material and would be pleased to receive any information that would enable us to do so:

The articles 'Copter Crashes' from the *Daily Express* 28th May, 1973, 'Racegoers Hurt' from The *Daily Express* 7th June, 1973 and 'Acid Alert' from The *Daily Express* 22nd June, 1973; The articles 'Motor-Bike Couple go Round The World' from The *Sunday Express* 17th June, 1973 and 'For The Kind Porter – £500' from The *Sunday Express* 6th May, 1973.

We are grateful to the following for permission to reproduce copyright photographs:

Associated Newspapers Ltd. for page 88; Associated Press Ltd. for pages 72, 80, 112; Barnaby's Picture Library for page 76; Daily Telegraph for page 52; Glasgow Herald & Evening Times for page 60; Inter-Continental Features for page 96; London Weekend Television for page 116; New York Times for page 120; Press Association for page 100; Sport & General Press Agency Ltd. for pages 44, 48; Sunday Times for page 68.

1

EAST ANGLIAN
DAILY TIMES
Saturday, April 7, 1973

Blaze shock for fire officer

SUB-OFFICER Jack Forman was shocked when he arrived at a Mildenhall caravan fire last night to find the blaze was at the home of his son David.

The fire was at Birchgrove caravan park, Folly Road.

Sub-Officer Forman said that action by neighbours had saved the caravan.

Mrs. Barbara Allsopp and mother of three, Mrs. Ann Everett, used buckets of water to prevent the fire spreading.

Filled buckets

Mrs. Allsopp said, "We were filling buckets of water from a tap with a fire extinguisher hanging above it. But we were so busy running backwards and forward with the water that we didn't notice it."

Despite their efforts, damage amounting to at least £300 was caused. Part of the caravan structure was burned, bed and bedding destroyed and other furniture badly scorched.

The caravan's owners, Mr. David Forman, 22, and his wife, Lesley, 20, who have been married six months, were out babysitting.

---

scorched (l. 30) turned brown by he[at]

1 Choose the best answers to these questions.

a Why was Jack Forman shocked when he arrived at the fire?
  a Because the fire was at night.
  b Because it was his son's home that was on fire.
  c Because he was not able to save the caravan.

b Was the caravan saved?
  a No, because the fire brigade arrived too late.
  b Yes, because a fire extinguisher was used.
  c Yes, because neighbours helped to fight the fire.

c Mrs Allsopp and Mrs Everett didn't use the fire extinguisher because
  a They didn't know how it worked.
  b They had no time to use it.
  c They didn't see it.

d Was the caravan badly damaged?
  a No, because Mrs Allsopp and Mrs Everett put the fire out.
  b Yes, although Mrs Allsopp and Mrs Everett put the fire out.
  c No, only a bed was burned.

e Where were the owners of the caravan during the fire?
  a They were sitting with their baby.
  b They were in the caravan.
  c They were not at home.

2 Sub-officer Jack Forman was *shocked*. (*l.* 1–2) Look at these ten adjectives, which have certain similarities in meaning, and at the ten sentences that follow them. Put each adjective into its appropriate sentence.

shocked   embarrassed   ashamed   furious
disappointed   worried   alarmed   puzzled
anxious   surprised

a Henry was _____ when the doctor told him that his wife was going to have triplets.
b Yes, I admit that I stole your purse and I am very _____.
c Mary Brown arrived at the party wearing a dress exactly like mine! I have never been so _____ in my life!
d I was kissing Daphne on the sofa; when Daphne's husband came in he was _____.
e My grandmother was _____ when I told her that I intended to marry a rich woman so that I would not have to work.
f I am _____ to know the results of the election. Have you any news?
g My wife was very _____ when I forgot her birthday.
h We have not had a letter from Alfred for over a month. I am _____. Do you think he is ill?

i Why on earth did he leave without even saying goodbye? I am
_____ by his behaviour.

j We were _____ to hear a shout of 'Fire! Fire!' during the night.

3 *Despite* their efforts, damage amounting to at least £300 was caused. (*l.* 25–27) This could also be expressed like this: Damage amounting to at least £300 was caused *although* Mrs Allsopp and Mrs Everett tried to save the caravan.

Rewrite these sentences, using *although* instead of *despite* or *in spite of*.

a In spite of the rain, we went for a swim.
b She married a pop singer, in spite of her parents' opposition.
c Despite my advice, my daughter has bought a scooter.
d Despite bad weather conditions, the yacht completed the course.
e In spite of the climate, I like living in London.

Now, rewrite these sentences, using *in spite of* or *despite* instead of *although*.

f Although I love her, I don't intend to marry her.
g He came to our party although he had broken his leg.
h Although Grandfather is ninety-three, he loves dancing.
i Although my wife objects, I am going to give up my job.
j I love you, although you are not perfect.

4 BLAZE SHOCK FOR FIRE OFFICER is the headline of the story. Write suitable headlines for these five stories.

a Mrs Martha Henderson, mother of three, was sent to prison for three months by Colthorpe Magistrates' Court yesterday, after having admitted breaking open the gas meter at her home, 17 Blair Street, Colthorpe, and stealing £11.45. This was only the most recent in a series of similar petty crimes, said Mr J. B. Wood, sentencing her. A prison sentence was clearly the only way to 'bring her to her senses'.

b During strong winds on Monday evening, a large tree crashed onto the house of Mr and Mrs Jack Straw, in Dinglefield Road, badly damaging the roof. Nobody was hurt, and it was lucky that Susan, the Straws' three-year-old daughter, was in her parents' room at the time, as her bed was covered with glass from a window which was broken in the incident.

c Not finding his car in the street where he had left it, Arthur Parker, of Leamington Avenue, phoned the police and reported it stolen. They came at once to investigate the matter, and, as they were writing down details, Mrs Doreen Parker, Mr Parker's wife, arrived in the car. She had taken it to go shopping, without telling her husband.

d The Hartlington Baby Show, which has been held in the village every summer for the last twenty years, will not take place this year. Miss Phyllis King, the organiser, said that there were so few children under the age of two that the show 'would not be worth while'.

e   A bridge is to be built across the River Mowle at Fringefield, to replace the hundred-year-old ferry. The ferryman, Bill Blowers, who has worked the ferry for forty-two years, is to retire. He said yesterday 'It's a pity that the old ferry has to go, but it can't cope with modern traffic'.

5 The story, as it is written, is just over 150 words long. Rewrite it, using not more than 50 words, for a second edition of the paper.

6

Clues across

1 The best part of the milk. Cats love it (5)
5 'Much Ado _____ Nothing' (Shakespeare) (5)
8 Rather stupid (5)
9 Not small (3)
11 Every (3)
12 If something is _____, you must have it (9)
16 Feminine of he (3)
17 Something to write with (3)
18 The remains of something burnt, or a tree (3)
19 Famous English university town (9)
23 Sick (3)
24 We must do this to live (3)

25 Some men like to go to a football _____, and some men use a _____ for a different purpose (5)
27 Generally, the sole of your shoe will wear out before the _____ (5)
28 A piece of wild, open countryside (5)

Clues down

2 What is left of a building after its destruction; sometimes only a few stones, but they can look romantic (4)
3 _____ proud _____ a peacock (2)
4 Some women are afraid of them (4)
5 Money that is given to the poor (4)
6 I don't like flying; I prefer to go _____ sea (2)
7 Opposite of beautiful (4)
10 Usual (7)
11 Organise (7)
13 Primitive sort of weapon: it is thrown (5)
14 Employ (3)
15 Timid (3)
19 You _____ to show your appreciation in a theatre (4)
20 Don't do that! I can't _____ it! (4)
21 Unpleasant feeling that makes you scratch (4)
22 The sun rises in the _____ (4)
25 Not you (2)
26 Not she (2)

2

'Copter crashes

NEW YORK, Sunday.—One man died and nine others were injured when a helicopter carrying Secret Service agents to guard President Nixon crashed into the Atlantic off Grand Cay, Bahamas, where he is holidaying.

DAILY EXPRESS
May 28, 1973

Racegoers hurt

One passenger was seriously injured and four others slightly hurt when a coach taking a party of Italians back to London from the Derby crashed into a fence less than a mile from the racecourse last night.

DAILY EXPRESS
June 7, 1973

PROPELLER HITS MAN

A man was taken to Wexham Park Hospital, Berkshire, with a broken arm yesterday after being hit by the propeller of a plane he was trying to start at White Waltham aerodrome, Berkshire.

DAILY TELEGRAPH
May 12, 1973

Acid alert

Police in Berkshire yesterday searched the road between Reading and Maidenhead for a container of sulphuric acid which fell from a lorry.

DAILY EXPRESS
June 22, 1973

12 British children injured in crash

Le Havre, May 29.—Twelve school children from Blackpool were slightly injured near here when the bus in which they were returning from Paris skidded on wet roads and ran into a house.

THE TIMES
May 30, 1973

1 Read the five short news paragraphs carefully, and then give *short* answers to the following questions.

  a Where was the helicopter going when it crashed?
  b How many people were hurt when the helicopter crashed?
  c How did the party of Italians go to the Derby?
  d How many of the Italian party were killed in the accident?
  e What was the man doing when his arm was broken?
  f How was his arm broken?
  g What were the police looking for between Reading and Maidenhead?
  h How had it been lost?
  i Where do the twelve British children live?
  j Why did their bus skid?

2 Now write questions, to which these ten phrases could be the answers.

  a (para. 1) nine
  b (para. 1) on holiday
  c (para. 2) London
  d (para. 2) Italian
  e (para. 3) the propeller of a plane
  f (para. 3) at White Waltham aerodrome
  g (para. 4) sulphuric acid
  h (para. 4) from a lorry
  i (para. 5) no, only slightly
  j (para. 5) by bus

3 Correct these statements.

  a The helicopter was carrying President Nixon.
  b The Secret Service agents were going to the Bahamas on holiday.
  c The coach that crashed was taking a party of Italian people to the Derby.
  d The coach crashed near London.
  e The man's arm was broken when his aeroplane crashed.
  f The propeller of the aeroplane was broken.
  g The container of sulphuric acid was lost in Reading.
  h Police found the container of sulphuric acid on the road.
  i The twelve British school-children had been visiting Le Havre.
  j The children were all badly injured.

4 Each of the five little news items is made up of a single sentence, but each sentence gives quite a lot of information. For example, the first sentence ('Copter Crashes) tells us:

> A helicopter has crashed – the helicopter was carrying Secret Service Agents – the Secret Service agents were going to guard President Nixon – President Nixon is on holiday at Grand Cay – Grand Cay is in the Bahamas – the helicopter crashed into the sea off Grand Cay – one man was killed – nine men were injured.

Now write similar *single-sentence* stories to give the following information.

  a A shop window was smashed – it was smashed by a bus – people in

13

the shop were covered with broken glass – two of the people were injured – one of them was taken to hospital – the bus was out of control – it was going down a hill – this happened yesterday afternoon – this happened in Beeton.

b   A valuable painting has been lost – it was lost yesterday afternoon – it was lost between London and St. Albans – it fell off a lorry – the picture was going to the Fusty Museum – its loss was discovered when the lorry reached St. Albans – the painting is valued at £500,000.

c   Miss Ruby Boston is ill – she is in hospital – she was taken to a London hospital yesterday morning – she had had a heart attack – she is an American singer – she is 45 years old – she was appearing at the Chat-of-the-City Club.

d   An engagement has been announced – the engagement is between Michael Johns and Lucinda Bust – Michael Johns is 25 years old – he is a famous footballer – Lucinda Bust is 23 years old – she is a model – she has been married before – her first husband was Lord Moneybags.

e   Mr George Smith is a Member of Parliament – he is 79 years old – he represents the town of Great Mucking in Parliament – he has represented Great Mucking for the last twenty-five years – he is going to retire – this will happen next year – he announced this yesterday – he is going to retire because of ill-health.

5

a   Police in Berkshire yesterday searched the road between Reading and Maidenhead for a *container* of sulphuric acid which fell from a lorry. (para. 4)

Here are some containers:

box	packet	jar	drum	bottle	tin
tube	bag	barrel	sack		

Put each of the following items into its appropriate container. For example: *matches* are contained in a *box*, so you write 'A box of matches'. (In some cases there is more than one possible answer – give as many as you can.)

matches	cigarettes	oil	toothpaste
peas	jam	marmalade	wine
beer	ink	honey	vinegar
cigars	envelopes	glue	rice
salt	mustard	chocolates	biscuits

b   Complete these phrases, choosing the words that are possible.

a bunch of flowers – keys – books – grapes – typewriters – dresses – bricks

a flock of priests – soldiers – sheep – fish – goats – children – ships

a set of	leaves – chairs – teeth – stamps – buses – books – tools
a suite of	rooms – relations – pigeons – music – furniture – cups – clothes
a pack of	bears – wolves – angels – chickens – cards – thieves – bees

c When we go shopping, we can buy a *bar* of chocolate – or a *slab* of chocolate. Fill in the missing words in these phrases.

a _____ of soap   a _____ of bread
a _____ of sausages   a _____ of cotton
a _____ of razor blades   a _____ of toilet paper
a _____ of cheese   a _____ of pearls
a _____ of wool   a _____ of writing paper

d Still on the subject of collective nouns, what are these? (Example: A crowd is a lot of men, women and children.) Try to give three examples for each, in the same way.

a Cattle are a lot of _____ _____ _____
b Poultry are a lot of _____ _____ _____
c Clothes are a lot of _____ _____ _____
d Furniture is a lot of _____ _____ _____
e Crockery is a lot of _____ _____ _____
f Cutlery is a lot of _____ _____ _____
g Seasonings are a lot of _____ _____ _____
h Stationery is a lot of _____ _____ _____
i Ironmongery is a lot of _____ _____ _____
j Drapery is a lot of _____ _____ _____

6 Episodes from the domestic life of George and Gaye Gambol appear every day on the back page of the *Daily Express*. Strangely enough, George and Gaye seem to be no older now than they were when they made their first appearance more than twenty years ago. Here is a typical 'Gambols' cartoon strip. Tell the story in your own words. Begin: One morning, Gaye found George standing beside the car in a very bad temper . . .

3

THE SUNDAY EXPRESS
London, June 17, 1973

MOTOR-BIKE COUPLE GO ROUND THE WORLD

TEACHER John Wise and his wife Dorreen who emigrated to Tasmania 12 years ago, decided to revisit England and see the world on the way— by motor cycle.

After driving 10,000 miles overland without even a puncture they have arrived in England.

They left Tasmania in January and now plan to stay for two months at Taunton, Somerset, where Mr. Wise's widowed mother lives in Hamilton Road.

Mr. Wise, 46. formerly science teacher at Askwith secondary school in Taunton, and his wife, who have three daughters. went to Hobart, Tasmania, in 1961.

Trust

For their return world trip Mr. Wise took a year's unpaid leave.

"We didn't have any spares with us," said Mr. Wise. "We just put our trust in ourselves and the machine."

So far the journey on a B.M.W. R50 through Australia, New Zealand. Panama. Mexico, the United States and Europe has cost £250 each.

Mr. and Mrs. Wise. now grandparents, plan to return through Europe, Asia and India, another 14.000 miles. They expect their final bill to be about £1.000.

1 Read the story carefully and then choose the best answers in this exercise.

a John and Dorreen Wise

    a used to live in England.
    b live in England now.
    c used to live in Tasmania.

b Their journey to England from Tasmania

    a was very long and tiring.
    b took about five months.
    c lasted a year.

c Their journey to Tasmania from England

    a will be quicker than the journey from Tasmania to England.
    b will be more expensive than the journey from Tasmania to England.
    c will be longer than the journey from Tasmania to England.

d During their journey

    a they had no trouble because they were well prepared.
    b they were very lucky to have no trouble.
    c they had a little trouble but nothing serious.

e The total cost of their journey is expected to be

    a about £500 each.
    b about £1,000 each.
    c about £250 each.

2 Teacher John Wise and his wife Dorreen who emigrated to Tasmania twelve years ago decided to revisit England and see the world *on the way*. (*l.* 1–6)

Fill the spaces in these ten sentences with expressions using *way*. Choose the expressions from this list.

       by the way   in the way   out of the way   wayside
       all the way   in a way   on the way   under way
       by way of   his own wa

a 'You look very tired.' 'Yes, I am. I couldn't get a lift and I had to walk _____.'

b Work is now _____ on the new bridge and they hope to have finished it by November.

c Mr and Mrs Wise came back to England _____ Mexico and the U.S.A.

d We stopped at a little _____ inn for the night.

e Quick! Get _____! A mad bull is coming!

f _____, did you notice what is on at the cinema?

g Would you please move your motor-cycle? It's _____. I can't get my car out of the garage.

h _____ I shall be very glad when the holiday is over.

i No, we aren't hungry. We stopped _____ to have a snack.

j If grandfather can't have _____ he gets very bad-tempered and irritable.

3 *After driving 10,000 miles overland without even a puncture they have arrived in England. (l. 8–11)* In this sentence, two ideas are combined:

They drove 10,000 miles overland without even a puncture. They have arrived in England.

Join these pairs of sentences in the same way, using *after* and making any changes that are necessary.

a We were able to buy three tickets for the concert. We waited an hour for the office to open.

b He passed his examination. He studied hard for six years.

c Uncle Joe worked hard for fifty years. He has now retired.

d Aunt Sally thought about driving for many years. She has at last bought a car.

e We reached the top of the mountain. We climbed for nearly six hours.

f He asked his father for some more money. He spent all the money he had.

g She could not see anything at all. She broke her glasses.

4 They *have arrived* in England. (*l.* 10–11) They *left* Tasmania in January. (*l.* 12–13)

Put the verbs in these sentences into the right tenses (present perfect or past simple).

a My friend Paul is in hospital because he (*break*) his leg; he (*break*) it last week, in a motor-cycle accident.

b I (*take*) a lot of photographs this year but none of them are as good as those I (*take*) last summer.

c Aunt Clara's bulldog (*bite*) me yesterday. I can't understand it, because he never (*bite*) anyone else.

d My brother (*write*) several novels, and last year he (*write*) a successful play.

e I (*tear*) my trousers on that chair yesterday. I really must have the chair repaired; it is the third pair of trousers I (*tear*) in three weeks.

f 'You ever (*ride*) a camel?' 'No, but I (*ride*) an elephant when I was in India.'

g Uncle Victor (*give*) me a very expensive present for my birthday last year. It surprised me very much, because he never (*give*) expensive presents to any of his relatives.

5 The headline to this story is **MOTOR-BIKE COUPLE GO ROUND THE WORLD.**

Write suitable paragraphs, of about 100 words each, for these headlines.

a WATER SHORTAGE HITS GARDENERS
b RECORD CROWD WATCH CHELSEA WIN
c RISE IN FARES PREDICTED FOR AUTUMN
d SMOOTH TYRES BLAMED FOR COACH CRASH
e PAY DISPUTE CLOSES CAR FACTORY

6 Imagine that you are either Mr or Mrs Wise. Write a first person account of your story (using only the information contained in the printed story), in about 150 words.

7

Clues across

1 When something is quite new and has never been used, we say that it is _____ new (5)
4 'There's no _____ like home' (5)
7 Sick (3)
8 Opposite of over (5)
9 Corner; a triangle has three, a square has four (5)
10 A measurement of weight – 2240 pounds (3)
12 William Tell was a Swiss _____ and Robin Hood was an English one (4)
15 The forty days before Easter (4)
17 Verb: to join together (5)
18 This may be used instead of braces (4)
20 The entrance to the garden (4)
23 If you are not yet 18, you are under _____ (3)
25 A good housewife will do this to her kitchen floor when it is dirty (5)
26 Flowers will do this if they do not have enough water (5)
27 A piece of wood, cut ready for burning on an open fire (3)
28 Your sister's daughter (5)
29 Opposite of friend (5)

Clues down

1 You may do this if you are embarrassed or shy (5)
2 The only poisonous snake to be found in Great Britain (5)
3 A good housewife does not like to see this in her home (4)
4 An architect may draw this (4)
5 To discuss (5)
6 Happening (5)
11 '_____ to the rain, the party was cancelled' (5)
13 December 24th is Christmas _____ (3)
14 Not in (3)
15 You have two; a table has four (3)
16 'To Have and Have _____' (Hemingway) (3)
18 You will find one in the bathroom (5)
19 Not small (5)
21 Opposite of below (5)
22 Not full (5)
23 I can = I am _____ to (4)
24 'The Razor's _____' (Somerset Maugham) (4)

4

THE DAILY MAIL
May 26, 1973

The first blackbird...

MRS Myra Webb, who was told by doctors that she would never hear again, lived for six years in a world of silence.

But yesterday she heard a blackbird sing in the garden of her home at Brighton, Sussex. 'My hearing is coming back—and its wonderful,' she said.

Mrs Webb, 26, claims to be the first woman in Britain to have her hearing restored by acupuncture, the needle therapy widely practised in China.

After six months' treatment she can listen to music again, carry on a conversation with the aid of a hearing aid—and has got a job as a typist with the South Eastern Electricity Board.

'It's marvellous to hear people talk,' she said at her home in Stanstead Crescent, Woodingdean, Brighton.

Mrs Webb began to lose her hearing at the age of 12 after a virus infection. 'By the age of 20 I had no hearing whatsoever.

'A friend told me about acupuncture and I went weekly for treatment. One night when I was in the kitchen I heard a faint sound and realised it was my musical kettle boiling. I went weak at the knees. My hearing has slowly improved since.'

Her husband David, a 26-year-old insurance worker, said: 'She is thrilled by the results and is continuing the treatment.'

1 *A blackbird* is the answer to the question 'What did Mrs Webb hear in her garden?'.

Write questions to which these phrases are the answers. (Use only information contained in the story.)

a six years
b 26
c by acupuncture
d a form of therapy using
   needles
e in China
f six months
g yes, she has, as a typist
h the South Eastern Electricity
   Board

i Brighton
j 12
k a friend told her
l her musical kettle boiling
m yes, but slowly
n an insurance worker
o David

2 Mrs Myra Webb was told by doctors that she would never hear again. (*l.* 1–4) The doctors said: 'Mrs Webb, you will never hear again.'

Now, complete these sentences in the same way.

a Mr Arthur Weaver was told by doctors that he would have to use a hearing aid. The doctors said: '_____.'

b The shop assistant told the customer that she was sorry the wallpaper he had ordered three weeks before hadn't arrived yet. The shop assistant said: '_____.'

c Freda Potts told her mother that she needed £2 to buy a new sweater to go with the skirt Aunt Mabel had sent her for her birthday. Freda Potts said: '_____.'

d The dentist's receptionist told Mrs Willoughby that the dentist would see her that afternoon at 3 o'clock if it was really urgent. The receptionist said: '_____.'

e My sister was told by a policeman that she could not park her car there on the corner of that street because a procession was coming along shortly. The policeman said: '_____.'

f My sister told the policeman that she was only leaving the car there for a few moments while she went into a shop to collect a parcel. My sister said: '_____.'

g Michael Duff was told by his boss that he might have to postpone his holiday because two other men in his division were sick. The boss said: '_____.'

h The postman told the housewife that there was a registered letter for her which he had not been able to deliver the previous day because there had been nobody at home. The postman said: '_____.'

i The dressmaker told Miss Bates that the material she had chosen was very attractive but that it wasn't suitable for a wedding-dress. The dressmaker said: '_____.'

j Vera Jamieson told her friend Betty that she couldn't go to the cinema with her because she had broken her glasses and she couldn't see without them. Vera said: '_____.'

3 *My hearing is coming back* (l. 11–12) is another way of saying 'My hearing is *returning*'.

Rewrite these sentences, using *come* with a preposition instead of the phrases in italics.

a '*Enter*' called the secretary when I knocked on the door.
b 'Has the patient *regained consciousness* yet, Nurse?' asked the doctor.
c It was a terrible experience, but we *survived* it with only minor injuries.
d My new book is *being published* next spring.
e I *found (by chance)* his address written on the back of an old envelope.
f 'How did you *get possession of* those diamonds?' asked the detective, suspiciously.
g It was a great *fall in dignity* for Aunt Bella to have to go by bus after being used to a big car and a chauffeur in uniform.
h 'Beryl has fainted, sir.' 'Well, throw some cold water over her. That will soon make her *revive*.'
i *Hurry up*, children, or we shall miss the train.
j Uncle John has left his wife and has run away with a policewoman? How extraordinary! How did that *happen*?

4 *The first woman in Britain to have her hearing restored.* (l. 15–17)

Examples: They employed someone to repair the broken windows
= *they had the broken windows repaired.*
I am going to tell the dentist to examine my teeth = *I am going to have my teeth examined.*

Rewrite these sentences in the same way.

a The people next door should get someone to cut their grass.
b You will have to ask someone to translate the article into Spanish and Portuguese.
c Do you think I look prettier? I have been to a doctor who straightened my nose.
d Uncle Leo paid someone to kill his wife.
e I am going to tell the hairdresser to dye my hair green.
f When I got a new passport, I had to ask a photographer to take a new photograph.
g We are paying some workmen to redecorate the whole house.
h I was employing a gypsy to tell my fortune when the bomb went off.

i Those curtains are very old and shabby. We ought to ask someone to make some new ones.

j 'This floor is very dirty, John. It needs sweeping.'
'Yes, sir, I will tell someone to do it at once.'

5 *It was my musical kettle boiling.* (l. 47–48)
What is a kettle for? A kettle is for boiling water in.

Now answer these questions in the same way.

a What is a watch for?	**f** What are scissors for?
b What is a saw for?	**g** What is a camera for?
c What is glue for?	**h** What is a hammer for?
d What is a suitcase for?	**i** What is a broom for?
e What is a drill for?	**j** What is a rubber for?

6 The story, as it is printed, is about 250 words long. Rewrite it, for a later edition of the newspaper, in not more than 100 words.

7 *Either* **a** Imagine you are David Webb. Tell the story of how your wife's hearing was restored.
or **b** Which is worse – to be deaf or blind? Write your own ideas in about 250 words.

8 Tell this story in your own words. Begin: One Sunday morning, George was going to work in the garden, but Gaye . . .

DAILY MAIL
September 10, 1971

Hospital collapses

By KEITH COLLING

A FULL scale inquiry began l a s t night after a partly built hospital extension collapsed in a tangle of smashed c o n c r e t e and twisted steel.

While experts sought the c a u s e 102 old people slept in a neighbouring identical building completed two months ago.

'We cannot see any reason to evacuate them to other premises,' said a spokesman for Birmingham Hospital Board which has charge of the extensions at Manor Hospital, Walsall, Staffordshire.

'We have every reason to believe that this (Bristol frame system) is a safe building design. But in the early stages it could be—we understand—possible for a very critical point to be reached during a high wind.

'This is not possible when the building is fully completed.

'So the old people will stay where they are.'

The collapsed unit, due to open in 1973, was the second stage of a £700,000 scheme to improve facilities for geriatric patients.

The collapse came during sharp wind gusts at

We trust design, says board, so old folk will not be moved

breakfast t i m e o n l y minutes. before teams of contractors were due to start work.

Workers' huts were crushed but no one was hurt.

It fell down 'like a pack, of cards,' said police.

The b u i l d i n g was designed by the architectural department of the Birmingham H o s p i t a l Board and Mr B. J. Dunn, assistant regional architect, said : 'It is too early yet to say what caused the collapse.

' 'As soon as the investigation is completed, rebuilding will start.'

An independent firm of structural steel engineers will lead the inquiry.

Mr Harry Griffiths. managing director contracted for both buildings, said : 'It's a complete mystery. High wind could have something to do with it.

'When my men packed up on Wednesday night everything was checked and found secure. We are waiting for a report from the consultant engineers.'

The framework was half finished to the top of the three-storey building.

When the structure fell it smashed a crane to pieces.

geriatric patients (*l*. 41) very old sick people

1 Read the news item carefully. Then choose the correct answers in the following exercise.

a We cannot see any reason to evacuate them to other premises (*l.* 15–17) means

  a we don't think it is necessary to move them.
  b we have no other accommodation to move them into.
  c we have not promised to move them somewhere else.

b Due to open in 1973 (*l.* 37–38) means

  a the building was planned to be ready for use in 1973.
  b the building was opened in 1973.
  c the building was a temporary one, planned to last only until 1973.

c To improve facilities (*l.* 40–41) means

  a to enlarge the building.
  b to make it easier to pay.
  c to make conditions better.

d It's a complete mystery (*l.* 71) means

  a there is something very mysterious about it.
  b it is very exciting and thrilling.
  c nobody knows the answer.

e A neighbouring identical building (*l.* 11–13) means

  a another part of the building that had collapsed.
  b a building like the one that collapsed, nearby.
  c another hospital in another town.

2 The news story is about a hospital building. Look at these words, all of which are connected with hospitals in some way, and then at the sentences that follow them. Put each word into its most appropriate sentence.

  maternity hospital   convalescent home   clinic
  ambulance   ward   operating theatre   sanatorium
  stretcher   surgery   mental hospital

a After her operation, she was sent to a _____ by the sea for six weeks.
b There were ten beds in the _____ but only eight of them were occupied at the time.
c We carried the unconscious boy down the hillside on a _____.
d I'd better go early; the doctor's _____ is always crowded on Monday evenings.
e He contracted TB while he was in the army, and spent two years in a _____ in the mountains.
f The poor man was so upset by his wife's death that he had to go to a _____ for treatment.
g There is a weekly _____ in our village for expectant mothers.

h With a screaming siren, the _____ rushed down the street in the direction of the hospital.

i They gave me an injection half an hour before I was taken into the _____.

j My wife went to the _____ for our first son, but all our other children were born at home.

3 *Sought* (l. 9) is the past form of *seek*. *Slept* (l. 11) is the past form of *sleep*. Put these sentences into the past form.

a My aunt weeps over the loss of her diamond necklace.
b He springs to his feet on the entrance of the great lady.
c Those animals breed very well in captivity.
d Frightened, she clings to her brother's arm.
e This singer broadcasts every Sunday afternoon.
f The escaped prisoner flees across the moor.
g Many people forsake the country to look for work in the town.

4 *Workers' huts were crushed* (l. 48–49) is a passive construction. 'The fall of the building crushed the workers' huts' is an active construction. But 'the fall of the building' is already understood as being the subject of the verb 'crushed' and it is not necessary to use it. The following sentences would be better expressed in the passive form. Change them, omitting the subject of the verbs.

a Some people are discussing the problem at this very moment.
b They are opening a new cinema in our town next week.
c Nobody can solve this problem.
d They had eaten all the food before I arrived.
e They will repair the telephone tomorrow.
f Someone knocked the old man down.
g They speak English in Australia.
h They may have moved it.

5 *As soon as the investigation is completed, rebuilding will start.* (l. 62–64) After expressions of time, like *as soon as*, it is not possible to use a future form of the verb. Present or present perfect forms are used instead. Other similar expressions like this are *when, after, until, before, as long as.* Put the verbs in these sentences into the right form.

a I (*telephone*) you before I (*arrive*).
b They (*paint*) the boat when they (*finish*) it; probably next week.
c As soon as I (*know*) the result of the tests, I promise you I (*let*) you know.
d She has gone to Spain, and (*stay*) there as long as her money (*last*).
e They (*carry on*) working until the bell (*ring*) in twenty minutes' time.
f After the holiday season (*begin*) all the hotels (*be*) full.

g They (*announce*) the departure of the train three minutes before it (*leave*).

h When he (*learn*) to work better he (*get*) better results.

i The doctor (*see*) you as soon as he (*come*) in.

6 This news item is just over 300 words long. Rewrite it for a second edition, in not more than 100 words.

7 Write a similar news story, of about the same length, on one of the following subjects, inventing whatever facts you wish.

a A collision between a goods train and an empty passenger train in a small country station.

b The collapse of a dam and the flooding of the surrounding countryside.

c The sinking of a ferry-boat.

Clues across

1 Big, huge, large, important (5)
3 Animals that give milk, and have the reputation of eating anything! (5)
6 Verb: to speak in a very quiet voice, almost without sound (7)
9 Heal (4)
10 Completely without feeling, like your mouth after the dentist has given you an injection (4)
11 Plural of is (3)
13 Mothers and fathers (7)
15 Insane, crazy (3)
17 'A friend in _____ is a friend indeed' (4)
19 What you feel if the dentist does *not* give you an injection! (4)
20 An Indian – the American kind (3–4)
21 Each (5)
22 It is dangerous to _____ on thin ice (5)

Clues down

1 Formerly Miss Kelly, now Princess of Monaco (5)
2 Very much like 19 across (4)
4 Not shut (4)
5 A Latin-American dance (5)
6 The paper around the goods that you buy in the shop (7)
7 When cutting sandwiches, the housewife _____ butter on the slices of bread (7)
8 Someone from Moscow, for example (7)
11 Nelson only had one (3)
12 Finish (3)
14 Serpent (5)
16 Verb: a noise you may make during your sleep! (5)
18 There are many varieties of this wild animal; some are to be found in England (4)
19 If you see elephants of this colour, you had better stop drinking! (4)

THE SUNDAY EXPRESS
May 6, 1973

FOR RESCUER RANDY — A SURPRISE ENDING

from **WEBSTER ANDERSON**
Toronto

RANDY DAOUST, 19, a bush pilot from Hay River in Canada's North-West Territories, rescued four campers who he said: "Looked like a bunch of bums."

He was delivering ice to a fish-packing operation when he spotted an overturned canoe on the Tolson River, south of Great Slave Lake.

After unloading his ice, he flew back to the river and spent four hours searching before he saw three men on an island.

He landed his float plane and taxied up. "They were in real bad shape," he said. "They had had nothing to eat for 10 days. They had been on a canoe trip and over-turned."

They told him a fourth man had become separated a few miles upstream.

Daoust found the man standing on the shore. "He was out of his head and didn't seem to want to come at first."

As he was flying the men out they told him that mosquitoes had been killing them " and they had decided to commit suicide—" They were that far gone."

Daoust left the men in Yellowknife and reported the incident. Two days later the men thanked him and left.

That was last summer and Randy Daoust has just found out that they were rich Americans who have set up a trust fund that will pay him £80,000 when he is 25.

For the kind porter—£500

Hall porter Jim Joy always had a helping hand for guests at the Dudley Hotel, Hove, Sussex. One guest, Miss Martha Dougherty, left him £500 in her will published yesterday.

Mr Joy said: 'She was short-sighted, so I helped her down the steps.' Miss Dougherty, in her eighties, left £150,899 net.

a bunch of bums (l. 6–7) a group of homeless people, vagabonds

float plane (l. 18) an aeroplane that can come down on water

out of his head (l. 30) delirious, crazy

1 *He was delivering* ice to a fish-packing operation when *he spotted* an overturned canoe. (*l.* 8–10) As *he was flying* the men out *they told* him . . . (*l.* 32–33)

Put the verbs in these sentences into the past simple or past continuous, as in these two examples from the story.

a When I (*wake*) the birds (*sing*) in the trees outside my window. I (*jump*) out of bed and (*run*) to open the window when I (*tread*) on a drawing-pin.

b While Freddie (*swim*) someone (*steal*) all his clothes.

c She (*work*) as a hotel receptionist when I first (*meet*) her.

d When Mr Simpson (*arrive*) home, he (*find*) that his wife (*have*) a party. People (*dance*) in the sitting-room, and more people (*sing*) in the dining-room. It was dark in the kitchen, so he (*not see*) what (*happen*) in there.

e As I (*cross*) the road a lorry (*knock*) me down and (*break*) my leg.

f The 'Titanic' (*sink*) in 1912 as she (*cross*) the Atlantic on her maiden voyage.

g I (*walk*) down Regent Street when a flower-pot (*fall*) on my head.

h I (*go*) into his room to wake him, but he already (*sit*) on the side of the bed; he (*put*) on his socks. When I (*wish*) him 'Good morning', he (*yawn*) and (*say*) he (*not want*) to go to work. When I (*tell*) him the sun (*shine*), he (*feel*) a little better.

2 *He was out of his head.* (*l.* 30) This is one of many idioms making use of the word *head.* Here are eight more. Put each one, in a suitable form, into its appropriate sentence.

> a head for heights   headlong   a good head for figures
> pig-headed   to head the list   headquarters
> to have one's head in the clouds   to get it into one's head

a She is a very impractical person; she always has _____ and never thinks about everyday matters.

b I was very proud to find that my name _____ of prize-winners.

c My wife usually helps me with my monthly accounts; she has _____ .

d We tried to persuade him to let us into the house, but he _____ that we were thieves and refused to open the door.

e She rushed _____ out of the room and we haven't seen her since.

f Uncle Rocco is so _____; he is convinced that he is always right, and will never take advice from anyone.

g No, thank you, I don't want to go up to the top of the tower, even if there is a magnificent view; I have no _____ .

h Can you please give me the address of the _____ of the National Coal Board?

3 *They told him that mosquitoes had been killing them.* (*l.* 34–35) This is indirect speech. They said: 'Mosquitoes were killing us'. This is direct speech.

Change these sentences from indirect speech to direct speech.

a She said that she had bought her little niece a pony for her birthday. She said: '_____.'

b They told me that they wanted to talk to me. They said: '_____.'

c Aunt Ethel said that her father had been a pirate. Aunt Ethel said: '_____.'

d He asked me to help him to repair the fence. He said: '_____.'

e They said that my tie didn't go with my suit. They said '_____.'

f She asked us if we had seen her Latin dictionary. She said: '_____.'

g He told us to be quiet and not to disturb the other students. He said: '_____.'

h They told us that they might come the following evening. They said: '_____.'

i Mrs Flowerdew said that she had fallen off her bicycle the day before. Mrs Flowerdew said: '_____.'

Now change these sentences from direct speech to indirect speech.

j Mr Trent said: 'I have never been to Spain but I went to Portugal last summer.'

k The little girl said: 'Would you please help me to put my suitcase on the rack, sir?'

l Uncle Percy shouted: 'Get out of my garden, you dirty little boys!'

m She said: 'Do you think this hat suits me, Brenda?'

n Brenda said: 'No, it makes you look like an elderly horse.'

o Mr and Mrs Beales said: 'We have been married for 45 years.'

p Margaret said: 'Where are my gloves, Agnes?'

q Agnes said: 'I don't know, Margaret. I haven't seen them.'

r He said: 'What is the time? My train leaves at half past six.'

4 They told him that *mosquitoes* had been killing them. (*l.* 34–35) Here are ten more insects. Put each one (in the singular or plural) into its appropriate sentence.

ant   fly   spider   butterfly   beetle   wasp
dragonfly   bee   moth   flea

a Quick! Give me my camera! There is a beautiful _____ with blue and green wings sitting on that flower. It will make a lovely picture.

b The best honey is made in June when the _____ collect the nectar from the acacia flowers.

c Don't sit down on the grass. There are a lot of _____ in this part of the forest.

d A huge _____ was hovering on the surface of the river, its wings practically invisible.

e Hundreds of _____ were buzzing around the body of the dead sheep.

f A big black hairy _____ hung by a thread from the ceiling above my head.

g Be careful when you pick fruit in the garden. There are a lot of _____ about this summer.

h We had to keep the windows closed at night because a lot of _____ came in, attracted by the light.

i I switched on the light, and saw that there were dozens of black _____ on the floor, scurrying away into the corners of the room.

j The dog has been scratching all the morning. Do you think he has _____ ?

5 *Daoust left the men in Yellowknife and reported the incident.* (*l.* 38–40) Here there are two verbs in the past tense – *left* (from *leave* – irregular) and *reported* (regular). Put these sentences into the past tense.

a They rise at 6.30.
b We buy fresh vegetables in the country.
c That cheese costs 75 pence a pound.
d The students raise their hands when they want to ask a question.
e I read a lot of magazines.
f Aunt Queenie flies to Colombo.
g We lay the table at seven o'clock.
h Mr Thompson digs his garden.
i She chooses smart clothes.
j The prisoner flees through the forest.
k Mrs Quinn writes for 'Belladonna' magazine.
l I tread on the ice very carefully.
m He spills coffee on his trousers.

6 The story 'FOR RESCUER RANDY – A SURPRISE ENDING' is about 220 words. Rewrite it for a second edition of the newspaper, in not more than 75 words.

7 Imagine that you are either Randy Daoust, or Jim Joy. Write about what you are going to do with the £80,000 (or £500) that you are going to receive. Do not write more than 300 words.

8 Tell the story in your own words. Begin: Gaye sometimes makes dresses for herself . . .

7

DAILY MAIL
December, 1973

Scientist warns of armchair blaze danger

A SCIENTIST warned yesterday of the fire danger in a type of foam upholstery widely used for furniture.

He said that within two minutes of a chair catching fire there would be flames 15ft. high. It would take only another minute to envelop an entire room.

Mr Kenneth Jones, principal scientific officer of the north-eastern forensic science laboratory told an inquest at Wakefield, Yorkshire : 'The spread of fire involving this material is incredibly and frighteningly fast and choking fumes are given off.'

He warned that it was a waste of time to try to put out this type of blaze. The best thing was to get out of the room and shut the door to prevent asphyxiation.

Verdict

Mr Jones said that in a house where a four-year-old boy died there was a three-piece suite with this polyurethane-ether foam filling.

He said: 'Some half million tons a year is produced, sufficient for 500 million armchairs.'

But the danger has been recognised and is being dealt with. A new product has just been developed in which the fire risk is reduced and will be available in a few months.

A verdict of accidental death was recorded on Richard Jolley, of Wakefield, who died in his bedroom from asphyxia.

upholstery (l. 3–4) covering, padding springs, etc., of armchairs and settees

forensic (l. 14) to do with the law

three-piece suite (l. 30–31) a set of two arm chairs and a settee of the same patter and colour

1 Read the news item carefully. Then choose the correct answers in the following exercise.

a Yesterday, a scientist said that certain types of armchairs

　a were widely used and upholstered.
　b might easily catch fire, because the materials used were dangerous.
　c should not be used because they were very dangerous.

b If an armchair of this type caught fire

　a things fifteen feet away would catch fire, too.
　b the whole room would be on fire within three minutes.
　c the fire would last three minutes.

c Mr Kenneth Jones was speaking at

　a the north-eastern forensic science laboratory.
　b a meeting of fire-prevention officers.
　c an inquiry into someone's death.

d Mr Jones said that with a fire of this kind

　a it was no use trying to put it out.
　b much time might be wasted.
　c it would take a very long time to put it out.

e Soon there will be a new filling for armchairs which will be

　a completely safe.
　b less likely to catch fire.
　c risky in case of fire.

2 A scientist *warned* yesterday of the fire danger in a type of foam upholstery. (*l.* 1–4)

Look at these ten verbs, which have certain similarities in meaning, and at the ten sentences that follow them. Put each verb into its appropriate sentence.

> warn　　advise　　threaten　　dissuade　　persuade
> remind　　hint　　scold　　recommend　　suggest

a I _____ you to study hard if you want to pass the examination.
b The spy _____ to shoot Miss James unless she gave him the information he wanted.
c The young man's father managed to _____ him from joining the army.
d Can I _____ you to buy a ticket for our next concert?
e Please _____ me that I have an important appointment at ten o'clock tomorrow.
f 'Don't _____ me, Mummy! It wasn't my fault!'
g They _____ that it would be better if we didn't ask any more questions.

h Can you _____ me a really good but cheap hotel?

i My sister _____ going to the cinema, but her friends had already seen the film.

j I _____ you that if you are late again you will be dismissed.

3 Now give the nouns from the same verbs. The first one has been done for you.

warn	= warning	remind	=	
advise	=	hint	=	
threaten	=	scold	=	
dissuade	=	recommend	=	
persuade	=	suggest	=	

4 Mr Kenneth Jones is _principal_ scientific officer of the north-eastern forensic science laboratory. (_l._ 12–15)

Look at these ten adjectives, which have certain similarities in meaning, and at the phrases that follow them. Put each adjective into its correct phrase.

principal   chief   main   best   champion
topmost   supreme   biggest   greatest   excellent

a A _____ road.
b The _____ branch of a tree.
c My _____ suit.
d An _____ dinner.
e The _____ tribesman.
f A _____ athlete.
g The _____ lake in the country.

h The _____ writer of this century.
i The _____ court.
j The _____ industries of the country.

5 Mr Jones said that within two minutes of the chair catching fire, there would be flames fifteen feet _high_. (_l._ 6–9) The _height_ of the flames would be fifteen feet.

Write the nouns from these other adjectives of size and dimension.

a high = height
b long =
c deep =

d broad =
e wide =
f thick =

6 A _three-piece suite_ (_l._ 30–31) would be found in a sitting-room. Make five columns, for _kitchen_, _sitting-room_, _dining-room_, _office_, and _bedroom_, and then put the following words into their appropriate columns.

wardrobe   desk   settee   armchair
dressing-table   coffee-table   sideboard
vegetable rack   refrigerator   chest of drawers

7 The word *furniture* is always singular, and needs a singular verb, although the meaning is plural. Other common words that behave in the same way are *information, advice* and *news.* Put the verb in these sentences into their correct forms.

   a The furniture that we bought in Singapore (*look*) lovely in our sitting-room.
   b The news (*be*) terrible last night, and I'm afraid it (*be*) even worse this morning.
   c That information (*not help*) me very much. Please tell me exactly what I must do.
   d My grandfather's advice always (*help*) when I don't know what to do.
   e Bad news always (*make*) my heart beat faster.
   f Good advice (*cost*) nothing.
   g That information (*answer*) my question. Thank you very much!
   h The new furniture just (*arrive*). Would you like to have a look at it?

8 He warned that it was a waste of time to try and *put out* this type of blaze. (*l.* 21–23) The verb *put* can be followed by other prepositions to give different meanings. Put suitable prepositions in the following sentences.

   a The Queen has had to put _____ her visit until next spring.
   b The last train has gone. Can you put me _____ for the night?
   c Put that vase _____ gently. It's very fragile and very valuable.
   d Don't forget to put the dictionary _____ on the shelf when you have finished with it.
   e Please turn the radio off! I can't put _____ _____ that terrible noise any longer.
   f When they reached the camping site, they put _____ their tents and went to sleep.
   g Don't shout at me like that! Put _____ your hand if you want to ask a question.
   h If you know the answer, put it _____ in your exercise book.

9 In the story, as it is printed, there are about 160 words. Imagine that you are news editor of the paper, and for your second edition you wish to use the same story, but now you have room for only 50 words. Rewrite the story, being careful to keep all the useful information and facts.

10 The headline of this story is SCIENTIST WARNS OF ARMCHAIR BLAZE DANGER. Choose one of the headlines below, and write a story of about 100 words that you think might go well under it.

   a 120 FIREMEN FIGHT ALL-NIGHT DOCKS BLAZE
   b GIRL'S 50-FOOT LEAP TO SAFETY
   c NEWLY-WEDS LOSE EVERYTHING IN CARAVAN FIRE

8

Boy, 14, rescued from cliff face

EASTERN DAILY PRESS
June 18, 1973

A 14-YEAR-OLD boy who last year had to be rescued by ladder after getting himself stuck at the top of a tree, was involved in an even more spectacular rescue on Saturday when he climbed up Hunstanton cliffs to get a closer look at a seagull and got stuck 40 feet up.

Hunstanton firemen and an ex–steeplejack from King's Lynn combined successfully to rescue the boy, Allen Peters, of 28, Queensway, Melton Mowbray, who was among a busload of young people who had come to Hunstanton on an outing organised by a Methodist Youth Club.

Allen said afterwards: "I was looking up at the cliffs and I saw a young seagull on a ledge so I thought I would climb up and have a look at it. I like birds. I looked after a pigeon once for quite a long time."

The first part of the climb was quite easy but after a bit it became more difficult and eventually Allen found that he could not get any higher. Worse still he realised he could not climb down again.

'SCARED'

"My foot kept on slipping on the sandstone," he said. "I was scared that I was going to fall so I just tried to keep still."

His friend, 13-year-old Ricki Sanches, of 15, Blakeney Gardens, Melton Mowbray, tried to help. He said: "I climbed up as far as I could but I couldn't get near him."

It was then that Mr. Ronnie Bramham, a plasterer, of 10, Kingsway, King's Lynn, became involved. Seeing the boy in difficulties he climbed up the cliff until he reached Allen, scraped out a couple of footholes for him and held on to him until rescue came.

Mr. Bramham said: "It seemed like half an hour. It would have been all right if I could have brought him down but once I got to him I realised I was stuck too. I wasn't worried about the height as I used to be a steeplejack."

By then the alarm had been raised and Hunstanton firemen drove across the grassy clifftop and parked a few feet from the edge. A rope was then lowered down.

Allen was lowered to safety first and Mr. Bramham a few minutes later. The whole incident lasted about 20 minutes and was watched by hundreds of holidaymakers enjoying a perfect summer's day on the beach.

Ricki said: "About a year ago Allen climbed right to the top of a tree in Melton Mowbray and they had to get a ladder to get him down."

Asked if he would do any more climbing Allen said: "I like climbing but I don't think I will climb anything made of that soft sandstone again. I couldn't get a proper grip."

steeplejack (l. 15) a man who climbs tall chimneys and towers to do repairs. (An 'ex-steeplejack' is a man who used to do this sort of work but now has changed his job.)

1 Read the news story carefully, and then give short answers to the following questions.

Example: How old was the boy who climbed up the cliff? Fourteen.

a What happened to the boy in 1972?
b What happened to the boy in June 1973?
c Does the boy live in Hunstanton?
d Why did the boy climb up the cliff?
e What did his friend Ricki do?
f Did Mr Bramham bring the boy down the cliff?
g Were Mr Bramham and Allen on the cliff for half an hour?
h Why was Mr Bramham not afraid of the height?
i How were they brought down?
j Why was the cliff so difficult to climb?

2 *Fourteen* is the answer to the question 'How old was the boy who climbed up the cliff?'. Write similar questions to fit these answers, using only information from the story.

a 40 feet
b Hunstanton
c the first part of the climb
d because he was afraid of falling
e a plasterer
f a steeplejack
g from the top of the cliff
h firemen
i a lot of holidaymakers
j probably, but not anything made of soft sandstone

3 My foot kept on *slipping*. (*l.* 43)
I just tried *to keep* still. (*l.* 46)
I like *climbing*. (*l.* 90–91)

Fireman and an ex-steeplejack combined *to rescue* the boy. (*l.* 14–18)

In these sentences, put the verb into the correct form – infinitive or gerund.

Examples: Would you consider (*lend*) me your car? = Would you consider *lending* me your car?
I helped her (*carry*) the trunk. = I helped her *to carry* the trunk.

a They have postponed (*take*) any decision until the end of next month.
b I am looking forward to (*meet*) your fiancée, but I can't help (*wonder*) why you have suddenly decided (*get*) married after all these years.
c Would you mind (*have*) a look in the bathroom to see if I remembered (*turn*) off the taps?
d Aunt Clara can't help (*cry*) when she sees a sad film, so whenever she goes to the cinema she always remembers (*put*) several large handkerchiefs in her handbag.
e (*lie*) in the sun is one of my favourite hobbies.
f He stopped (*talk*) (*listen*).

37

g I could not stop (*talk*) when I saw you yesterday morning as I was late for work.

h It's no use (*try*) to open that drawer; it's locked and I can't find the key.

i I remember (*see*) that film on television sometime last year.

j Uncle Methusalah put off (*make*) a will until he was 107 years old.

k I have nothing to do this evening because our teacher forgot (*give*) us any homework.

l Stop (*look*) at me like that; I couldn't help (*stand*) on your foot. The bus is so crowded.

m I wish the baby next door would leave off (*scream*). It hasn't stopped (*cry*) since last Friday.

n I don't feel like (*work*) this morning; let's go to the beach.

o I don't advise (*take*) those pills. They were prescribed for the horse when it was ill.

p I don't mind (*work*) hard all the week, but I refuse (*work*) on Sundays.

4 *Seeing the boy in difficulties he climbed up the cliff.* (*l.* 56–58) This is another way of saying 'He climbed up the cliff because he saw the boy in difficulties'.

Rewrite these sentences in the same way.

a I telephoned for the police because I heard a woman scream.

b She didn't light a match because she smelled gas.

c I wrote a cheque and went to the bank because I had no money in the house.

d They would not sleep in the castle because they were afraid of ghosts.

e He couldn't answer the question because he didn't know the answer.

f I didn't jump into the river to rescue the child because I can't swim.

g Johnny can't go to the football match because he must visit his sister in hospital.

h Helen didn't go to work yesterday because she felt ill.

i We were able to open the box because we hit it with a hammer.

j She didn't go to see the film with us because she had already seen it.

5 Hunstanton firemen drove across the *grassy* clifftop. (*l.* 71–72)
A clifftop *covered with grass* is a *grassy* clifftop.

Rewrite these phrases in the same way, replacing the words in italics with an adjective.

Example: A contract that can be renewed is a *renewable* contract.

a a day *on which it rains a lot*

b a person *whom it is possible to like*

c a man *who easily gets irritated*

d a look *which is full of meaning*
e hair *which is so white that it looks like snow*
f a face *which has not been shaved*
g circumstances *which were not foreseen*
h cheese *which has a strong smell*
i food *which cannot be eaten*
j a chair *which can be folded up*
k a ladder *which can be extended*
l news *which is so strange that you can't believe it*
m a bell *that warns people about something*
n a person *who is so unpleasant that you cannot bear him*
o an idea *that is so stupid that an idiot might think of it*

6 Imagine that you are Ricki Sanches. Tell the story of Allen's adventure, and the part you played in it. Use about 200 words.

7

Clues across

1 Boy's name (5)
4 Passageway between the seats in a church or a theatre (5)
7 Clever (11)
9 It may cover a saucepan (3)
10 Say (4)
13 A friend; especially in wartime (4)
15 Hurt (5)
16 It gives light (4)
18 You may make one with your girl-friend, or eat one from a tree! (4)
21 A necessity for all English people at 5 o'clock (3)
23 Pence and halfpence are, but fivepence pieces and tenpence pieces are not (6,5)
24 It rises from boiling water, and it may scald you (5)
25 You may find this on the beach (5)

Clues down

1 To float with the current of the water (5)
2 Absolutely necessary (5)
3 The weather may be this – lessons may be this too! (4)
4 Not sweet (4)
5 If you can't do this, you will have great difficulty with dictation (5)
6 Opposite of exit (5)
8 May be used instead of matches (7)
11 Historical period (3)
12 Once round the race-track (3)
13 Opposite of subtract (3)
14 Not a little (3)
16 Used to fasten shoes (5)
17 The leaf of this tree is the national emblem of Canada (5)
19 If you are not this, you are dead! (5)
20 An artist puts his canvas on this when he paints; a teacher may put a blackboard on it (5)
21 The school year is usually divided into three of these (4)
22 Deeds (4)

Two injured by blast in caravan

TWO men on a touring holiday of Britain were injured by an explosion in their motor caravan in the centre of Norwich yesterday.

Shoppers, traders and businessmen in Red Lion Street were startled by a loud bang, and seconds later the two men leapt from the vehicle, which had stopped outside Barclays Bank.

Several people rushed to give assistance and helped to put out the fire inside the vehicle, a light American truck converted to provide living accommodation, before Norwich firemen arrived.

TREATMENT

The men — American Mr. Gary Houser, aged 25, of Ohio, who was driving, and his passenger Mr. Charles Lynn, 23, of Vancouver — were taken to Norfolk and Norwich Hospital with minor burns.

They were allowed to leave after treatment.

"I heard this explosion. It was pretty loud, I thought it could have been a bomb," said Mr. Leslie Webster, deputy clerk of the markets, who was working in his office in Red Lion Street.

"I looked out of the window and saw this chap leap from the van and roll on the pavement.

"Then another chap came out of the van. He seemed to be in a worse state—parts of his trousers were hanging in shreds below his knee.

"I came downstairs to get a fire extinguisher, but by the time I got outside someone from the bank was in the van with an extinguisher."

Mr. Webster, who lives at 71, Trinity Street, Norwich, said both victims were shocked. One was taken into the markets office to await an ambulance.

"The second man insisted on going back into the van to see if everything was all right, and five minutes later he came out with a drawer that was blazing," he added.

The explosion was also heard inside the bank. Staff provided a fire extinguisher and telephoned for an ambulance.

Although a plastic window was blown out, damage inside the vehicle was mainly superficial.

The two men have spent the last six months touring the Continent and had travelled to Norwich from Snetterton. At the time of the incident their wives were shopping in the city.

hanging in shreds (l. 47) torn or cut in small pi

1 Read the news story carefully, then choose the best answers in this exercise.

a The two men in the caravan were

    a slightly hurt.
    b badly injured.
    c shocked but unhurt.

b Mr Webster thought that the explosion

    a was a bomb.
    b wasn't a bomb.
    c was like a bomb.

c Mr Webster didn't take a fire extinguisher to the caravan because

    a he couldn't find one.
    b someone else got there first.
    c there wasn't one in the bank.

d In the explosion

    a the windows of the bank were blown out.
    b the caravan was burned.
    c the contents of the caravan were damaged.

e The two men were

    a working in Norwich city centre.
    b waiting for their wives.
    c on holiday.

2 *Shoppers, traders and businessmen in Red Lion Street were startled by a loud bang, and seconds later the two men leaped from the vehicle, which had stopped outside Barclays Bank.*

This is a compound sentence, made up of the following separate ideas:

Shoppers, traders and businessmen were startled. These shoppers, traders and businessmen were in Red Lion Street. A loud bang startled them. Two men leapt from the vehicle. This happened seconds later. The vehicle had stopped outside Barclays Bank.

Now, combine each set of ideas into *one* compound sentence, as in the example. You may have to change the order of the ideas, or the wording, slightly, but your sentence must contain all the information given.

a Two goals were scored. The first goal was scored by Smith. The second goal was scored by Jones. These two goals were scored during the first ten minutes of the game.

b The condition of children's teeth today is very good. It is better than it has ever been. The Minister of Health said this. He said it in the House of Commons. He said it yesterday afternoon. He was speaking in a debate. The debate was on hospitals.

c Six people were killed. Another fourteen people were injured. This happened when two trains collided. They collided yesterday. They collided outside Jayton station. One train was a goods train and was empty. One train was a passenger train. It was crowded.

d The price of butter is going up next week. This announcement was made yesterday. This announcement was made by a government spokesman. Butter has already gone up twice this year. The price was increased by 1p per pound in February. The price was increased by 1p per pound in June. The new increase will be of ½p per pound.

e Some drugs and medicines are very dangerous. They are especially dangerous for small children. These drugs should be kept out of the reach of small children. The best place for this is a cupboard. It should be possible to lock the cupboard. The cupboard should be high. The children should be too short to reach the cupboard.

3 Two men on *a* touring holiday of Britain were injured by *an* explosion in their motor caravan in *the* centre of Norwich yesterday. (*l.* 1-7)

Put *a*, *an*, *the* in the spaces in these sentences, if necessary.

a _____ mathematics is _____ subject that I hate _____ most of all at _____ school. I can never remember _____ right way to deal with _____ fractions, and _____ logarithms are _____ complete mystery to me.

b _____ first time I saw _____ Thames I was very disappointed. I had expected to see _____ very wide, majestic river, full of_____ crystal clear water, with _____ beautiful houses on _____ banks. But I went to _____ south of London, to _____ dock area, where _____ water is very dirty, and _____ warehouses between _____ London Bridge and _____ Tower Bridge look like _____ dirty grey prisons.

c _____ woman came to _____ door yesterday and tried to sell me _____ encyclopaedia. She said that it would be useful for _____ education of my children. When I told her that _____ youngest of my children was twenty-five years old, and was in _____ army, she tried _____ different argument, and told me _____ silly story about preparing myself for _____ leisure I would have after _____ retirement.

d 'You need _____ six-week holiday, Mr Powell.'
'But, Doctor, I can't possibly leave _____ office during _____ busiest period of _____ year.'
'That's _____ nonsense, Mr Powell. _____ health is far more important than _____ work.'
'Should I follow _____ diet, too, Doctor?'
'You should eat _____ salad and _____ fresh meat, which are good for _____ liver and help to cure _____ digestive disorders.'

e   _____ life of _____ teacher can be _____ very contented one, if _____ students he teaches are receptive. But _____ success of _____ job depends not only on _____ intelligence of _____ students but also on _____ imagination and _____ patience of _____ teacher. _____ really good teacher is _____ man or _____ woman who could not be really happy doing anything else.

4 The second man *insisted on going* back into the van. (*l.* 59–60)

Following this example, complete the following sentences, using the verb given and the necessary preposition.

a Are you looking forward – (*start*) your new job?
b Aunt Phoebe is thinking – (*emigrate*) to New Zealand.
c Will you please refrain – (*make*) that dreadful noise?
d We are counting – (*see*) you at our party next week.
e Nurse Gordon has been given a medal. She jumped into the river and rescued a man – (*drown*).
f We take great pride – (*produce*) high-quality goods.
g When Paul leaves school, he wants to go – – (*act*).
h The low-lying land along the river banks is prone – (*flood*).

5 Imagine that you are one of the men in the caravan. Write a first-person account of your adventure in Norwich. Do not use more than about 250 words.

6 The headline for the story is TWO INJURED BY BLAST IN CARAVAN. Write suitable short stories for the following headlines.

a ONE DEAD THREE HURT IN AFTER-PARTY CRASH
b FAMOUS STAR'S DEATH FALL
c MEAT UP AGAIN: RUN ON FISH
d HONEYMOON ARREST: GROOM DENIES CHARGES, BRIDE IN TEARS
e RAIL FARES TO BE CUT

7 Tell the story in your own words. Begin: George and Gaye have a nephew and niece called Flivver and Miggy. They are very naughty children, and whenever they come to stay with the Gambols they manage to get into mischief. One day Gaye went shopping . . .

Italy Finally Defeats U.K. In Soccer

TURIN, June 14 (AP).—Italy defeated England tonight for the first time in 40 years, scoring a 2-0 victory in an exhibition
5 game which meant a lot to the pride of Italian soccer.

A sellout crowd of 70.000, filling the Turin Municipal Stadium, saw Italy's first victory over
10 England in nine games. The eight previous games ended in four victories for England and four ties.

Center-forward Pietro Anastasi
15 put Italy ahead at the 38th minute. Inside-right Fabio Capello scored Italy's second goal. at the 52d minute. Both Capello and Anastasi play for Italian cham-
20 pions Juventus of Turin.

The game celebrated the 75th anniversary of the foundation of the Italian Soccer Federation in this north Italian industrial
25 city. It was also the world record 107th game with the English national team for its captain Bobby Moore.

In the closing minutes, the
30 English missed two good chances to score. Even Moore tried to shell the Italian goal from far out.

The play became a little bit
35 rough and the referee booked Englishman McFarland.

to shell (l. 31–32) to shoo
booked (l. 35) wrote his n
in a book (because he
committed an offence)

1 Read the story carefully, and then give *short* answers to the following questions.

a   Who won the football match?
b   How many goals did England score?
c   How many goals did Italy score?
d   Where was the game played?
e   How many people watched the game?
f   When was the Italian Soccer Federation founded in Turin?
g   Who is Bobby Moore?
h   How many times has Bobby Moore played for England?
i   When did the English team have two good chances to score?
j   Why was McFarland booked?

2 ... which meant a lot to the *pride* of Italian soccer. (*l.* 5–6)

Pride is the abstract noun from the adjective *proud*. Give the abstract nouns that come from the following words.

a   hate   f   likely
b   vacant   g   recognise
c   dislike   h   remember
d   poor   i   possible
e   true   j   wealthy

Now, write sentences using these abstract nouns.

3 Fabio Capello scored Italy's second goal. (*l.* 16–17)

Rewrite these phrases using the *'s* form, *where possible*.

For example: The hat of my brother = my brother's hat.
             but 'The top of the mountain' cannot be changed into this form.

a   the toys of the children   k   the ideas of Mr Lucas
b   the middle of the street   l   a wait of five minutes
c   the leg of the table   m   the blue of the sky
d   the leg of the horse   n   the bicycle of Fred
e   the colour of the flower   o   the heat of the sun
f   the clothes of Aunt Alice   p   the yacht of the millionaire
g   the clothes of the 19th century q   for the sake of heaven
h   a holiday of a month   r   the schools of the state
i   the end of the journey   s   the blanket of Linus
j   the bottom of the hill   t   the wing of the bird

4 Both Capello and Anastasi play for Juventus. (*l.* 18–20)
Capello plays for Juventus. Anastasi plays for Juventus = Both Capello and Anastasi play for Juventus.
Capello doesn't play for Inter. Anastasi doesn't play for Inter = Neither Capello nor Anastasi plays for Inter.
Join these sentences in the same way, using *both* or *neither*.

a Marlon Brando is an American actor. Steve McQueen is an American actor.
b Roses grow in England. Tulips grow in England.
c Vinegar is not sweet. Lemon juice is not sweet.
d I am not rich. My brother is not rich.
e We can't come to the picnic. They can't come to the picnic.
f Sheila doesn't play tennis. Eleanor doesn't play tennis.
g Picasso was Spanish. Goya was Spanish.
h The wine in that part of the country is very good. The food in that part of the country is very good.
i Algebra is a very useful subject. Trigonometry is a very useful subject.
j Shakespeare didn't write novels. Wordsworth didn't write novels.
k Butter has gone up in price recently. Margarine has gone up in price recently.
l I didn't understand the lecture. My friend Pamela didn't understand the lecture.
m Uncle Matthew doesn't smoke. His wife doesn't smoke.
n Wood is used in the manufacture of modern furniture. Plastics are used in the manufacture of modern furniture.
o George didn't come to my party. His wife didn't come to my party.
p November is a very cold month in England. December is a very cold month in England.
q The butcher hasn't sent his bill this month. The baker hasn't sent his bill this month.
r Betty doesn't drive. Marie doesn't drive.
s Cows eat grass. Sheep eat grass.
t Lake Garda is very beautiful. Lake Como is very beautiful.

5 *Italian* is the adjective from the noun Italy. Give the adjectives from these nouns.

a	Argentina	k	Portugal
b	Peru	l	Czechoslovakia
c	Hungary	m	Yugoslavia
d	Thailand	n	Vietnam
e	Belgium	o	New Zealand
f	Iceland	p	Mexico
g	France	q	Chile
h	Brazil	r	Panama
i	Jamaica	s	Switzerland
j	Scotland	t	Pakistan

6 Read the story again, and then write a similar account, in not more than 200 words, of any interesting sporting event you have seen

or

Explain why you like your favourite sport.

7

Clues across

1 Verb: to change (5)
4 Opposite of right (5)
7 'I must give you the money that I _____ you' (3)
8 'What was the _____?' you may ask at the end of the match (5)
11 What a priest does to the people (5)
14 'Either Jane _____ her sister will come' (2)
16 Abbreviation, meaning 'on behalf of', often seen at the end of business letters (2)
17 Between your shirt and your skin! (9)
18 _____ proud _____ a peacock (2)

19 Not out (2)
20 A history scholar (9)
23 'I love you. Do you love _____?' (2)
24 You may do this when you see the lights change to green (2)
26 Stranger; more curious (5)
29 Verb: to hold tightly (5)
31 Modern form of thou (3)
32 You should always _____ things after washing them (5)
33 'The winds have _____ over the ocean, And brought back my bonnie to me' (5)

Clues down

1 Too (4)
2 Also (3)
3 Eggs of a fish (3)
4 A spider makes one to trap flies (3)
5 Singular (3)
6 You will do this if you dive into very cold water! (4)
9 Broken, under a heavy weight (7)
10 _____ for danger (3)
12 Something untrue (3)
13 Part of a car, or inside an armchair (7)
15 Used instead of a bullet in ancient times (5)
21 Not he (3)
22 Not well (3)
23 Othello was one (4)
25 Not closed (4)
27 Loud, unpleasant noise (3)
28 One kind of corn (3)
29 A young wolf, lion, tiger or bear (3)
30 Queen Victoria died more than seventy years _____ (3)

11

'£1m' JADE STOLEN IN MAYFAIR

DAILY TELEGRAPH
June 16, 1973

By JOHN WEEKS
Crime Staff

A CHINESE jade figure of a rhinoceros, claimed to be worth about £1 million, has been stolen

5 with other valuable antiques, from the Mayfair home of Mr David Edge, 65, a fine art collector, it was revealed yesterday.

10 The robbery took place while Mr Edge was at his home in Tangier. He also has homes in Marakesh and Egypt.

Mr Edge, wearing a cream

15 kaftan with gold edging, and yellow pointed slippers, told me last night: "A writer friend, Raoul Balin, who visits my apartment when I am away

20 phoned me in Tangier at Easter and told me there had been a robbery."

Mr Edge returned from Tangier on June 1, but did not

25 report the theft to police until Thursday "because I was too ill even to lift a telephone."

Best piece

Mr Edge, who was attended

30 by a Moroccan manservant, went on: "The jade rhinoceros is about 10in long. It must be worth £1 million as it is the best piece in my collection.

35 "I have had it for about 20 years, but cannot remember exactly where I bought it or how much I paid."

The world record auction

40 price for jade is £71,000. This was paid for a 14in long figure of a water buffalo at Sotheby's in March. But Mr Edge says that a piece of jade similar to

45 his stolen rhinoceros, was sold in New York 11 years ago for £500,000. Neither the jade rhinoceros nor the other valuables were insured.

Mr David Edge surrounded by the rest of his collection of antiques in his Mayfair flat yesterday.

jade (*l.* 1) precious stone, usually green

kaftan (*l.* 15) a long loose kind of dress, of Turkish origin

1 Read the news item carefully, and then choose the best answers in this exercise.

a Mr Edge
  a has four homes.
  b usually lives in Tangiers.
  c only lives in London in the winter.

b The robbery
  a took place yesterday.
  b was discovered by the police.
  c happened some time before Easter.

c Mr Edge
  a paid £1 million for the jade rhinoceros.
  b says his jade rhinoceros was sold for £500,000.
  c thinks his rhinoceros is worth £1 million.

d A 14 inch long jade figure of a water buffalo
  a was sold for a high price in March.
  b is the most valuable piece of jade in the world.
  c was the best piece in Mr Edge's collection.

e Mr Edge
  a was in New York eleven years ago.
  b collects antiques.
  c is an artist.

2 *A Chinese jade figure of a rhinoceros, claimed to be worth about £1 million, has been stolen with other valuable antiques, from the Mayfair home of Mr David Edge, 65, a fine art collector, it was revealed yesterday. (l. 1–9)*

This compound sentence contains nine pieces of information:

1 a figure has been stolen
2 the figure was made of jade
3 the figure was Chinese
4 it was a figure of a rhinoceros
5 it was in the home of Mr Edge
6 Mr Edge lives in Mayfair
7 Mr Edge is 65 years old
8 Mr Edge is a fine art collector
9 this news was revealed yesterday

Now write similar compound sentences to combine the following sets of information.

a An aeroplane crashed yesterday. It crashed near Blackpool. It was a small aeroplane. It was a private aeroplane. The aeroplane belonged to Mr George Owen. Mr Owen is 36 years old. Mr Owen lives in Manchester. Nobody was injured. The aeroplane was badly damaged.

b Mrs Martha Edwards is the mother of Paula Edwards. Paula Edwards is a famous actress. She acts in films. She won an award at the Cannes Film Festival. The Cannes Film Festival took place last month. Paula Edwards has given her mother a necklace. The necklace is made of diamonds. The necklace was a birthday present.

c Two children were injured yesterday. The children were aged 5 and 7. They were playing in a garden. It was the garden of their parents. A lorry crashed through the fence of the garden. The brakes of the lorry had failed.

d Patricia Austin is a famous soprano. She has been singing with the Cosmopolitan Opera for the last sixteen years. She announced yesterday that she is going to retire. She is going to retire next October. She wants to spend more time at home. She has a husband and three children.

3 *Mr Edge was wearing a cream kaftan with gold edging and yellow pointed slippers. (l. 14–16)*

In the following sentences, all about clothes, there are some blanks. Fill these spaces choosing your words from the following list:

shoes	stockings	skirt	suit	hat	braces
dress	vest	scarf	trousers	jacket	collar
gloves	belt	underpants	artificial	blouse
sleeves

a She had a long woollen _____ round her neck, and a warm _____ pulled down over her ears. But she had no _____ on and her hands looked blue with cold.

b I have grown so much thinner that I cannot keep my _____ up without the help of a _____ or a pair of _____.

c She dressed very carefully for her first day at her new job. She put on a white silk _____ with long _____ and a high _____, a smart black gaberdine _____, and a pair of black leather _____.

d 'You really must buy a new _____, John. You can't go to Ann's wedding wearing that awful dark grey one you bought for Uncle Joe's funeral.'
'Can't I wear my new check _____ and fawn _____? They are very smart.'
'For a country walk, perhaps, but not for a fashionable wedding!'

e 'Why are you running around the house in your _____ and _____?'
'Because I can't find a clean shirt or a pair of trousers.'

f Before nylon was invented, _____ were usually made of silk, or _____ silk.

50

4 *Neither the jade rhinoceros nor the other valuables were insured* (l. 47–49) is another way of saying 'the jade rhinoceros was not insured and the other valuables were not insured'.

Join these sentences in the same way. (Notice that when both the nouns are singular, the verb is singular too. For example: *Mary was not at home and Anne was not at home* becomes 'neither Mary nor Anne *was* at home'.)

a Butter is not as cheap as it used to be. Eggs are not as cheap as they used to be.
b I don't speak Chinese. My wife doesn't speak Chinese.
c The police have not been informed. The press has not been informed.
d I shall not be at the party. My friend Angela will not be at the party.
e Ostriches can't fly. Penguins can't fly.
f She didn't tell me her name. She didn't tell me where she came from.
g You can't have any notes. You can't have a dictionary.

5 *Mr Edge was wearing a cream kaftan.* (l. 14–15) The word *cream* has the same vowel sound as *been*. Here are fifteen words, with the *ea* vowel combination. Underline the words that have the same sound as *been*.

mean	head	deaf	bread	dream	clean
cheat	dread	heat	sweat	beat	dead
realm	steam				

The word *rhinoceros* has the accent on the second syllable rhi*noc*eros. Underline the accented syllable in these words, which all have four syllables.

ridiculous admirable nevertheless
understanding necessary beneficial avoidable
photographer memorable satisfaction
preparation believable absurdity superfluous
adorable

Tell the story in your own words. Begin: When George and Gaye go to the supermarket by car . . .

12

Chinese acrobats of brilliant charm

By FERNAU HALL

DAILY TELEGRAPH
July 5, 1973

IT was a rare experience to attend a show at once so innocent, so charming, so skilled, and so fresh as that given at the Coliseum by the Shanghai Acrobatic Theatre.

Many of the items were familiar in character.

They were similar to those shown in the West in circuses and on variety stages. There were trick cyclists, high-pole acrobats, jugglers and so on.

But even these acts had a character all their own, because of the Chinese music, the delightful projected settings of Chinese country scenes, and the obvious joy and ease of the performers—all young, with an average age of 23.

But the most fascinating items were those that were distinctively Chinese, with traditions going back thousands of years.

Of all such items, the most delightful was the opening number, in which two giant red lions danced. These lions were each performed by two men inside the skin, but they worked together so perfectly in harmony that they gave a convincing illusion of an actual animal dancing with great skill, and sometimes showing an engaging sense of humour.

In fact all the items had a certain element of dance emerging in the smooth, elegant movements of the performers and also in the poses taken up by them from time to time.

Such moments aroused vivid memories of the unforgettable visit to London in 1955 of the "Ching-Chi" (Peking Opera from the People's Republic of China): the links with the traditional Chinese acrobatic numbers and some aspects of "Ching-Chi" were quite clear.

acrobats (headline) entertainers who perform difficult and spectacular gymnastic movements

jugglers (l. 12) entertainers who can manipulate a lot of balls, plates, bottles, etc., in the air, without letting them fall

1 Give short answers to the following questions.

a What was particularly rare about this show, according to the writer?

b In which theatre are the Chinese acrobats appearing?

c Are all the items completely new to English audiences?

d Which were the most interesting items in the programme, in the writer's opinion?

e Are all the performers under 23 years old?

f Which item did the critic enjoy most?

g Did real lions appear in the opening number?

h Why did the performance of the acrobats make the writer think of the Ching-Chi?

i What happened in 1955?

j What was the writer's general opinion of the show?

2 It was a rare experience to attend a show at once so *innocent*, so *charming*, so *skilled* and so *fresh*. (*l.* 1–3) In the show there was such innocence, such charm, such skill and such freshness.

Rewrite these sentences, using nouns in place of the adjectives or adverbs that are in italics, and making any other changes that are necessary.

Examples: He acts so *realistically* that his performance is completely convincing. He acts with such realism that his performance is completely convincing.

How *wide* is the street? What is the width of the street?

a She talks so *candidly* that most people dislike her.

b Mr Sharples is such an *able* teacher that his students get on very quickly.

c Uncle Charlie shouted at me so *angrily* that I was quite terrified.

d It is already established that he is *famous*.

e 'The fact that the prisoner is *young* must be taken into consideration,' said the judge.

f How *deep* is the pool?

g Many *heroic* deeds were done during those unhappy months.

h I can't put up with such *childish* behaviour any longer.

i The occasion was so *gay* that everyone managed to forget his troubles.

j The photograph is so *dark* that it is difficult for me to recognise anyone in it.

3 It was a rare experience to attend a show so fresh as *that* given at the Coliseum. (*l.* 1–3) Many of the items were similar to *those* shown in the West in circuses. (*l.* 6–9)

In these two sentences, the words *that* and *those* have been used to avoid repetition of *show* and *items*. Using *that, those,* or *the one,* rewrite these sentences in the same way to avoid repetition, making any necessary changes.

a   I have never ridden in such a comfortable car as the *car* my Aunt Minnie drives.
b   There were many famous pictures in the exhibition; the *pictures* by Renoir and the *pictures* by Manet aroused the most interest.
c   City clothes are more formal than the *clothes* worn at the seaside.
d   The speech made by the President's wife was far more entertaining than the *speech* made by her husband.
e   Few novels are now more widely read than the *novels* written by Charles Dickens.
f   This house is very similar to the *house* I was born in.
g   My brother's new girl-friend isn't as attractive as my cousin's *girl-friend*.
h   Skirts nowadays are much shorter and more attractive than the *skirts* that were worn when Aunt Hilda was young.
i   The cigarettes in the red packet are milder than the *cigarettes* in the yellow one.

4   It was a rare experience. (*l.* 1) Experience has the accent on the second syllable: ex*pe*rience. Acrobats (headline) has the accent on the first syllable: *ac*robats. Acrobatic (*l.* 4) has the accent on the third syllable: acro*ba*tic.

Underline the accented syllables in these words.

development   comfortable   satisfactory   analyse
popularity   notwithstanding   avenue   particularity
picturesque   commercial   magnificent   manageable
perpendicular   parallel   horizontal   sympathy
sympathetic   upholstery   immediately   successful

5   It was a *rare* experience. (*l.* 1)

Look at these ten words, which have certain similarities in meaning. Then read the sentences that follow, and put each word into its appropriate sentence.

unusual   new-fangled   extraordinary   odd
seldom   sparse   scanty   unorthodox   peculiar
scarce

a   The kangaroo and the kiwi are both _____ to Australasia.
b   'I don't like these _____ zip-fasteners,' grumbled Grandfather, as he struggled to put on his trousers.
c   My uncle holds some very _____ views on marriage, religion, medicine and politics.
d   There was little rain during the spring, and the vegetation is very _____ this summer.

54

e The _____ swim-suits that you can see on the beaches today would have shocked our grandparents.

f Helen Keller was both blind and deaf, and yet she became a famous writer; this was a most _____ achievement for a person with such a handicap.

g Hurricanes _____ occur in this part of the world.

h I like your shoes. They are most _____. Where did you buy them?

i I thought Kate's behaviour at the party was rather _____.

j Good apples are very _____ this year.

6 Write a similar review, of about 250–300 words, of any show that you have seen and found particularly interesting, *or* in about the same number of words describe *one* aspect of the folk-culture of your country (music, dancing, etc.)

7

Clues across

1 Verb: to make a book or a picture (5)
4 Verb: to let the liquid run out, from a glass or cup, for example; usually by accident (5)
7 _____ do you do? (3)
8 Opposite of lower (5)
9 Verb: let, permit (5)
10 With which you hear (3)
11 The doctor may feel it in your wrist (5)
14 A little foggy; not very clear (5)
17 Verb: to cut off (5)
20 If it stops beating you will die! (5)
23 Used for cutting down trees (3)
24 The same (5)
25 Verb: to avoid something by making a quick, twisting movement (5)
26 I don't believe you! You are pulling my _____! (3)
27 Stock of money (this expression is often used in card games) (5)
28 Mistake (5)

Clues down

1 Rather fat (5)
2 Verb: to drive forward (5)
3 More than two and less than four (5)
4 A very large number of bees (5)
5 The British _____ (5)
6 Humble (5)
12 'Your sheets are so white, Mrs Jones. Which washing powder do you _____?' (3)
13 Verb: to take legal action against someone (3)
15 I have (3)
16 Sticky, black stuff; used for making ships waterproof and for mending roads (3)
17 Verb: to say (5)
18 Arch; especially that of a roof (5)
19 A driving competition for a large number of motorists or motorcyclists (5)
20 You may find it around a field or a garden (5)
21 A snake (5)
22 Of them (5)

13

THE GUARDIAN
Thursday, April 5, 1973

'Stolen' car had been buried

By our Correspondent

Mr and Mrs John Dawn were tired of the trouble their car was giving them, so Mr Dawn drove it to a building site in Wales where he worked and buried it with a mechanical digger. His wife, Linda, then reported to the police that it had been stolen and tried to claim £400 from their insurance company.

The couple appeared before South Shields magistrates yesterday charged with trying to obtain £400 from the National Insurance and Guarantee Corporation Ltd by deception.

Mrs Dawn (27), of the Opencastle caravan site, Cannock, Staffordshire, admitted the offence, but Mr Dawn (29), of the same address, denied it. The case against him was proved.

Mr Terry McGowran, prosecuting, said that the couple bought their seven-year-old Wolseley in 1972 on hire purchase. On February 17 Mrs Dawn reported to Sunderland police that the car was stolen. It was worth £400 and she claimed to the insurance company.

Mr McGowran said : " The car was later found in the middle of Wales in a tip near a roadworks. It was a mangled heap of machinery resembling the remains of a motor vehicle." The numberplates had been removed, but the engine and chassis numbers were still there.

Mr Dawn worked on the site at Dinas Mawddwy, near Glamorgan, driving bulldozers, but he had been seen driving a mechanical digger on the site although he had no authority to do so.

In a statement to the police Mrs Dawn said that her husband had telephoned her from Wales and told her that he had got rid of the car so she reported it stolen to police in Sunderland and made a claim

Mr and Mrs Dawn were each fined £100 and ordered to share court costs of £47.25.

hire-purchase (*l.* 29–30) a method of paying for something. A deposit is paid, and then a number of monthly instalments until the complete price (plus the interest) has been paid

tip (*l.* 38) a place where rubbish is deposited

1 Read the news item carefully. Then choose the best answers in this exercise.

a Mrs Dawn told the police that

    a her husband had buried their car.
    b that someone had stolen their car.
    c that their car was worth £400.

b Mr and Mrs Dawn

    a paid £400 for their car.
    b wanted to sell their car for £400.
    c had a car worth £400.

c Mr and Mrs Dawn wanted to get rid of their car because

    a it was insured for £400.
    b it wasn't a very good car.
    c it was seven years old.

d Mr Dawn's job was

    a driving bulldozers.
    b driving mechanical diggers.
    c building.

e *a* Mr and Mrs Dawn were both found guilty.
    b Mr Dawn was found guilty but his wife not.
    c Mrs Dawn was not prosecuted.

2 Mr Dawn drove it to a building *site* in Wales. (*l.* 3–5) Look at these ten words, which have certain similarities in meaning, and at the ten sentences that follow them. Put each word into its appropriate sentence.

> place   location   site   position   zone
> neighbourhood   premises   plot   territory   land

a When I retire I want to live in the country, and I have already bought a _____ of land by the sea where I am going to build a house.
b This hotel is built on the _____ of an old monastery.
c The police have not yet been able to find the exact _____ of the crime.
d It is regarded as a _____ of great natural beauty, and people often come here to paint.
e My grandfather's house stood in a very exposed _____, on the top of a hill.
f The _____ between the two frontiers is No-Man's-Land.
g The 'Green Dragon' is the most popular pub in the _____.
h No unauthorised people are allowed on the _____.
i The plains are arable _____ but the hills are not cultivated.
j Those islands are still British _____, but they will probably become independent soon.

3 *His wife, Linda, then reported to the police that it had been stolen.* (l. 7–9) This is a passive construction. Linda Dawn could also have reported to the police that 'somebody had stolen the car'. (This is an active construction.)

Change these sentences from the passive to the active.

a   The case against him was proved. (l. 24–25)
b   The car was later found in the middle of Wales. (l. 36–38)
c   The numberplates had been removed. (l. 42–43)
d   He had been seen driving a mechanical digger. (l. 49–50)
e   Mr and Mrs Dawn were each fined £100. (l. 60–61)

Now put these active sentences into the passive form.

f   What a dreadful noise! It sounds as if someone is killing a pig!
g   They will have to pull down that old house.
h   They may have cancelled the flight.
i   Someone always used to wake me up at 5.30 when I was in the army.
j   They deliver the post very early in the morning.

4 *Their seven-year-old Wolseley* (l. 28–29) is a convenient way of saying that their Wolseley car was seven years old. Write similar phrases to express the following ideas.
Examples: A pole which is ten feet long = *a ten-foot-long pole.*
A man with blue eyes = *a blue-eyed man.*

a   a house with four storeys
b   a book that is bound in leather
c   a boat with a glass bottom
d   a story which has been written well
e   a sandwich that someone has eaten half of
f   a man whose voice sounds angry
g   a store where customers serve themselves
h   a woman who looks delicate
i   a child who has been brought up well
j   a wall which is six feet high

Can you explain the following expressions?

a   a down-to-earth sort of person
b   a down-in-the-mouth expression
c   a cat-and-dog life
d   a holier-than-thou attitude
e   a cut-and-dried decision
f   a never-to-be-forgotten experience
g   a peaches-and-cream complexion
h   a couldn't-care-less attitude
i   a forget-me-not
j   a stick-in-the-mud

5 *Mr Dawn worked on the site at Dinas Mawddwy, near Glamorgan, driving bulldozers, but he had been seen driving a mechanical digger on the site although he had no authority to do so.* (l. 46–52)

This is a compound sentence, expressing the following ideas: Mr

Dawn worked on the site. The site was at Dinas Mawddwy. Dinas Mawddwy is near Glamorgan. His work was driving a bulldozer. He had been seen driving a mechanical digger on the site. He had no authority to do this.

Now, express these groups of ideas as compound sentences.

a The President arrived at the airport. He thanked the reception committee for their kind words. He said he was glad to be back in the country again. He said sadly, that his visit to the United Nations Organisation had not been as successful as he had hoped. He said he would be making a full report to Congress later.

b Jones scored in the last five minutes of the second half. This brought the score to 2–2. However, the game was not over yet. Theobald managed to slam home a glorious goal. This happened in the very last minute of the game. This made it a victory for Bollingham Rovers.

c Timmy Dowd has not been seen since Monday evening. Timmy Dowd is six years old. He left home on Monday evening at six o'clock. He was going to the sweet-shop. The sweet-shop is only three doors away from his home. He wanted to spend a 10-pence piece. His uncle gave him the 10-pence piece.

d There has been an epidemic of cholera. This epidemic alarmed the population of the whole country. This happened last month. It has now been brought under control. This is thanks to the prompt action of the medical authorities in Westwich. Westwich is a small town in the Midlands. The disease first broke out in Westwich.

e There was a mysterious explosion. It happened yesterday. It happened at Felton House. Felton House is the headquarters of the Anti-People Party. A parcel had been left. It had been left in the entrance hall. The parcel exploded. The receptionist was slightly injured. Several windows were broken.

6 The news story is nearly 300 words long. Rewrite it for a second edition, using not more than 100 words.

7 Tell this story in your own words. Begin like this: When Gaye bought a new dress . . .

59

14

Six firemen die searching for colleague

THE DAILY TELEGRAPH
August 26, 1972

SIX of seven Glasgow firemen who died in a warehouse fire yesterday were searching for a trapped colleague, police disclosed last night.

5　They were killed when the blazing roof of a textile warehouse in Kingston crashed down on them at the height of the fire. Police said that shortly after firemen entered the building there was a "blow-out" of

10　flames on the top floor.

"Two firemen were injured and a third was trapped. The two injured firemen were removed to the Victoria Infirmary,

15　said the police.

The spokesman **added**: "Meantime, a rescue squad of six, equipped with breathing apparatus, entered the building

20　searching for trapped fireman. There was a further blow-out the roof fell on the rescue squad, trapping them."

Emergency meeting

25　Mr William S. Gray, Lord Provost of Glasgow, called an emergency meeting of the city's Police and Fire Committee for today. Questions are expected

30　to be asked about whether the firemen—all wearing breathing apparatus—stayed in the warehouse after it was clear that civilians were safe.

35　The Lord Provost said last night: "I am assured that the police committee are going to look very seriously at the question of fire prevention."

40　In November, 1968, 22 people died in a blaze at a furniture factory in Glasgow. In March, 1969, 19 firemen and members of the Glasgow Salvage Corps

45　died in a whisky warehouse fire.

Of the seven firemen who died five were married.

civilians (l. 34) ordinary people (not firemen)

1 Read the story carefully and then give *short* answers to the following questions.

- **a** How many firemen died in the fire?
- **b** Where was the fire?
- **c** How many firemen were trapped in the building?
- **d** What were the other firemen doing when they were killed?
- **e** Who were taken to hospital?
- **f** Why did a special squad of six firemen go into the building?
- **g** Who has called a meeting for today?
- **h** What is the purpose of the meeting?
- **i** Who is the Lord Provost of Glasgow?
- **j** What happened in November 1968?

2 *Glasgow* is the answer to the question 'Where was the fire?'. Now write questions to which these phrases might be possible answers.

- **a** when the roof collapsed
- **b** one of them was
- **c** police did
- **d** two were
- **e** because the building was full of smoke
- **f** no, only firemen
- **g** all six were
- **h** yes, very seriously
- **i** in a furniture factory
- **j** no, it was in a whisky warehouse

3 *The firemen who died were searching for a lost colleague.* (l. 1–3)
This sentence gives the following pieces of information: Some firemen died. This happened while they were searching. They were searching for a colleague. The colleague was lost.

Now write similar compound sentences giving the following sets of facts.

- **a** Some nurses became ill. This happened while they were working. They were working in a department of the hospital. It was the X-ray department.
- **b** Some spectators got wet. This happened while they were sitting. They were sitting near one end of the swimming pool. It was the deep end.
- **c** Some books were stolen. These books were kept in a cupboard. The cupboard was locked.
- **d** Some thieves were caught. This happened while they were driving. They were driving a car. The car was stolen.
- **e** Some farmers emigrated. They emigrated because they were looking for some land. The land was farming land. It was more fertile.

f Some swimmers were drowned. This happened while they were trying to cross a river. The river was running very swiftly.

g Some dogs woke up all the neighbours. They did this by barking loudly. They were barking at an intruder. The intruder was wearing a mask.

h Some policemen were injured. This happened while they were trying to rescue someone. They were trying to rescue a boy. The boy was trapped in a building. The building was burning.

i Some pictures were damaged. This happened while they were being examined. They were being examined by a firm of experts. They were art experts.

j Some plates were broken. This happened while they were being carried into the kitchen. They were being carried by a maid. The maid was clumsy.

4 The story is about firemen. *A fireman is a man who fights fires.* Write similar definitions for the following.

a	milkman	k	witness
b	postman	l	shepherd
c	foreman	m	journalist
d	dustman	n	tailor
e	night-watchman	o	chauffeur
f	bandsman	p	caretaker
g	footman	q	clown
h	cameraman	r	jockey
i	customs man	s	miner
j	policeman	t	greengrocer

5 The headline of the story is SIX FIREMEN DIE SEARCHING FOR COLLEAGUE. Say in a few words what you think the following headlines would be about.

a FOUR NURSES HURT IN HOSPITAL BLAZE
b HUNDREDS OF CATTLE DIE IN FLOODS
c TWINS FOR TV STAR
d HEADMASTER TO RETIRE
e OVERDUE SHIP FEARED LOST
f BALCONY COLLAPSES: BABY INJURED
g AIRPORT STRIKE: HOLIDAY PLANES DELAYED
h SHEEP KILLED: DOGS FEARED
i NEW ROOF FOR CATHEDRAL AFTER 500 YEARS
j FOUR SMUGGLERS ARRESTED ON BEACH

6 The story is written in about 240 words. Rewrite it, for a second edition of the newspaper, in not more than 80 words.

7 Write a similar news report on one of the following topics:

a The flooding of a low-lying part of a town during heavy rain.

b Damage to a town or a village caused by an earthquake.

c A mountaineering accident.

8

Clues across

1 The Royal Academy of Dramatic Art teaches students to _____ (3)

4 Past of bite (3)

6 'Take your coat _____ and sit down' (3)

9 Opposite of tight (5)

11 This is not strange (5)

12 Your secretary may sit on it, but don't tell your wife! (3)

13 'If at first you don't succeed, _____, _____ again!' (3) (3)

14 The colour of the centre traffic light (5)

17 You may go to see one at the theatre (4)

18 Too (4)

20 It comes in winter (5)

21 Old-fashioned second person singular (4)

23 Draw a margin at the _____ of the page (4)

25 Lights (5)

28 Every (3)

30 Opposite end of your foot from your heel (3)

32 Unpaid worker, not free to leave (5)

33 Not dirty (5)

34 '_____ do you do?' (3)

35 What you want to do when you are tired (3)

36 Two _____ two are four (3)

Clues down

1 '_____ the world's a stage' (3)

2 Used before cars were invented (5)

3 'Room at the _____' is a famous novel (3)

4 A ray of light, a smile, or a support for the roof (4)

5 Melody (4)

6 Opposite of in (3)

7 The conductor asks: 'Any more _____?' (5)

8 Present form of flew (3)

14 Very unpleasant (5)

15 When there are flowers on it, a plant is in _____ (5)

16 Taxes that British householders pay (5)

17 Past of 35 across (3)

19 Half of two (3)

22 Familiar greeting (5)

24 Cry of pain or distress (5)

26 Years and years (4)

27 Agreement in trade or politics (4)

28 What is left after fire (3)

29 The police are officers of the _____ (3)

30 Something to drink (3)

31 This clue comes at the _____ (3)

15

DAILY MAIL
Thursday, May 10, 1973

No school for 50 motorway children

FIFTY children are being kept at home because their parents say the journey to school is too dangerous.

Daily Mail Reporter

5 The parents acted when a special coach service was withdrawn.

The coaches took 160 children, aged 8 to 12, across the M3 from Lightwater, Surrey, to school at

10 Bagshot. When a subway was built under the motorway, Surrey County Council said the children could walk.

But parents say this is too dangerous as the children have to cross

15 a busy roundabout to get to the subway.

Mr John Roberts, an electrical engineer and father of two, of Mount Pleasant Close, Lightwater, is chair-

20 man of an action group. He said yesterday: 'Many of us will keep our children away from school until we can ensure their safety. We have staged protest marches and sent

25 deputations.

'But they have refused to reinstate the coaches. Presumably, a child has to be killed or seriously injured on the way to school before any action

30 is taken.

'On the first day of term last week, 87 children were kept away and there are still over 50 at home.

'No children are going to school

35 from Lightwater without escort and those kept at home are being given tuition together at various houses.'

Surrey Education Committee will have a report on the situation at their

40 meeting next week.

A spokesman said yesterday: 'The children concerned live within the two mile limit of the school and are not entitled to special coach travel.

45 Since September 1971, this was provided as a temporary measure.

'No action has yet been considered in respect of children being kept away from school by their parents.'

M3 (*l.* 8) a motorway in the south of England, between London and Southampton

1 Read the news item carefully. Then choose the best answers in this exercise.

a Why are the children being kept at home?

    a Because the school is a very long way from their homes.

    b Because their parents say that it is not safe for them to go to school.

    c Because a child has been killed on the way to school.

b Why were the coaches stopped?

    a Because there were not enough children.

    b Because the parents protested.

    c Because a subway was built.

c *a* All children of school age in Lightwater are staying at home.

    b A lot of school children in Lightwater are staying at home.

    c Children aged from 8 to 12 are staying at home.

d *a* Lightwater parents have asked the council to reinstate the coaches.

    b Lightwater parents have asked the council to build a new school.

    c Lightwater parents have refused to let their children have lessons.

e Which children are entitled to special coach travel?

    a Those living further than two miles from the school.

    b Those living on the other side of a motorway.

    c Those who live in Lightwater and go to school in Bagshot.

2 *The journey to school is too dangerous.* (l. 3–4) This can also be expressed as 'The journey to school is not safe enough'.

Rewrite the following sentences, using *too* instead of *enough*.

a This fruit is not sweet enough to eat.

b That knife is not sharp enough to cut wood.

c I'm afraid you are not wealthy enough to marry my daughter.

d Please turn up the radio. The music is not loud enough for me to hear.

e This material is not fine enough to make a good filter.

f They didn't work well enough to win a prize.

g Molly Malone isn't tall enough to be a policewoman.

h Glass is not nearly flexible enough to use for this job.

Now rewrite these using *enough* instead of *too*.

i The school is too far away to walk to.

j Aunt Minnie is too slow to understand that joke.

k Many of the shops in Geeton are too expensive for ordinary people like me.

l Be careful! The coffee is too hot to drink.

m Uncle Barney is too stupid to find a good job.

n This street is too narrow for big lorries to go along it.

o That fabric is too rough to use for underwear.

p The new soldiers were too frightened to ask the sergeant if they could sit down.

q This pen is too thick to write neatly with.

3 *Fifty children are being kept at home.* (*l.* 1–2) This is a better way of saying 'They are keeping fifty children at home'.

Rewrite these sentences in the same way.

a They are discussing the matter at this very moment.

b When I arrived, they were getting my room ready.

c They are wearing hair shorter and curlier this year.

d They are pulling down those old houses behind the station.

e When we telephoned they were already operating on him.

f Your trousers are nearly ready, sir; they are just pressing them.

g They were reading out the list of prizewinners when she came in.

h They are finding new remedies every day.

i They are digging a new canal from Elton to Emham.

j They were singing the National Anthem when I left.

4 *The parents acted when a special coach service was withdrawn.* (*l.* 5–6) The two sentences 'The parents acted.' 'A special coach service was withdrawn.' can be joined in this way, or like this: 'When a special coach service was withdrawn the parents acted.' However, if we join the sentences like this: 'A special coach service was withdrawn when the parents acted', the meaning is completely changed.

Join these sentences, using *when*, in the most logical way.

a Someone looked out of the window. I knocked at the door.

b Her husband died. She sold the house.

c Aunt Nellie bought a new bicycle. Her old one was stolen.

d She pressed the button. The machine started.

e Uncle Tom opened the box. A mouse jumped out.

f The train stopped. She got off.

g We went indoors. It started to rain.

h They went home. The film ended.

i Egbert stopped throwing mud at the windows. I told him to.

j She put on her winter clothes. The weather grew colder.

5 A *motorway* is a main highway linking big cities. Here are the names of some other sorts of communications. In the following sentences, fill in the blanks with the appropriate word.

> road   avenue   street   lane   alley   path
>
> drive   pavement   way   cul-de-sac

a It's a very busy _____, with a lot of traffic, trams in the centre, and several pedestrian crossings, as it is right in the shopping centre.

b When I was a child, we were very poor and lived in a dilapidated old house in a narrow _____ between two factory buildings.

c From the front gate, a wide _____ sweeps up to the main door of the house.

d The _____ through the woods is very pretty, but be careful you don't stray from it; it isn't very well marked.

e An excellent _____ has just been built, linking all the resorts along the coast.

f Aunt Martha lives in a very elegant _____, which is very wide and lined with trees.

g This is a _____; there is no way out at the other end.

h The _____ was crowded with shoppers, and it was difficult to avoid stepping into the street.

i It's only a _____, very muddy, and not really wide enough for a big car like yours.

j Can you tell me the _____ to Deeton, please?

6 What are the special traffic problems of your town, or neighbourhood? How have they been solved? Or how do you think they should be solved? Write your ideas, in about 250 words.

7 Tell the story in your own words. Begin: For their holiday this year, George and Gaye went . . .

16

SUNDAY TIMES MAGAZINE
November 4, 1973

THE QUICK BROWN FOX AND THE LAZY DOG

By George Perry
Photograph by Barry Lategan

Tag is plainly a fox. Merlin is a foxhound. They should be adversaries. But instead they are the closest of friends. When Tag was a
5 tiny cub he was found dying in the woods after the rest of his litter had been exterminated. The people who rescued him put him with an old bitch who had just whelped, and he
10 was raised with the pups. Merlin, the smallest and the last of the litter, became his special friend and together they made a team to take on the rest of the kennels. But the day
15 came when Tag had to go back into the wild, and Merlin had to learn to hunt in the pack. It was then that both animals had serious problems adjusting to what were supposed to
20 be their natural roles.

The story is an unusual one. Originally *The Belstone Fox* was a novel by David Rook; it has now been filmed by James Hill (he
25 directed *Born Free*, which would mean that he knows something of putting together animal pictures). The film opens in London at the Odeon, Leicester Square on Thurs-
30 day. It took two years' hard work, and the animal actors had to be raised exactly as they were in the book. When reunited, here, they licked each other enthusiastically.

The key human is Asher Smith, 35 the professional huntsman to the Belstone hounds, a man who is a master of his trade, yet who quietly reared the foxcub in his kennels. Eric Porter plays Asher. 40

Anti-foxhunting factions will look in vain for a propaganda platform in the film, which, very impartially, details the workings, not of a fashionable hunt, but of a workaday 45 one, in a documentary manner. "I was totally neutral about foxhunting when I started the film," said Porter. "Now I think that if you have got to kill foxes, and they really do have 50 to be kept down, then hunting them is the best way to do it"●

bitch (*l.* 9) female dog – in this case, a female foxhound
whelped (*l.* 9) gave birth

1 In line 1, *a fox* is the short answer to the possible question 'What is Tag?'. Here are some more short answers, based on the story of Tag and Merlin. Write questions to which these could be the answers.

a	a foxhound	i	David Rook
b	no, but they should be	j	James Hill
c	very well indeed	k	'Born Free'
d	in the woods	l	Thursday
e	dying	m	enthusiastically
f	with foxhound pups	n	in his kennels
g	Merlin did	o	hunting
h	they had to leave each other		

2 He was *raised* with the pups (*l.* 9–10) could also be expressed as 'He was *brought up* with the pups'. In the sentences that follow, replace the phrasal verb with a single verb.

Example: Luckily the bomb didn't *go off*. Luckily the bomb didn't *explode*.

a Miss Bramble didn't *turn up* until nearly half past ten this morning.

b We hope that the film will *bring in* a lot of money.

c 'Good morning,' I said, 'I'm very sorry . . .' 'Never mind about that,' *cut in* Mr Carter. 'Now that you're here you'd better start work.'

d Please *ring up* before nine o'clock, or after dinner in the evening.

e I'm going to *do out* the attic on Saturday. Will you help me?

f 'You really must *look over* what you have written before you send letters out, Miss Jones,' Fred told his new secretary.

g The fire was only a small one and it was soon *put out* by the Fire Brigade.

h I am very much afraid that rents and fares will *go up* again in the autumn.

i My dog loves *running after* cats.

j '*Take off* your dirty shoes before coming in,' ordered Mrs Burton 'and leave them in the porch.'

3 *Eric Porter plays Asher* (*l.* 40) can be expressed equally well in the passive form 'Asher is played by Eric Porter'. But not all sentences can be expressed equally well in both forms.

I love you is obviously better than 'you are loved by me' (which is ridiculous). But *that beautiful picture was painted by a child of thirteen* is better than the active form ('a child of thirteen painted that beautiful picture') because we wish to stress that it was a child who painted the picture.

In this exercise, change the sentences into the passive form if necessary. Indicate which are better in the active form, and which it is impossible to change.

a   My grandfather built the house that we live in.
b   James Hilton, not A. J. Cronin, wrote 'Lost Horizon'.
c   Uncle Harry bought a bicycle last week.
d   I came as quickly as I could; somebody told me about it only ten minutes ago.
e   The new hospital, which the Queen opened last month, is the most modern in Britain.
f   A small girl read the poem, which was long, very difficult and full of strange words, beautifully.
g   Fishermen in the islands make these lovely, intricate little models of ships.
h   Beryl Childers, aged sixteen, of Church Lane, Cobblesham, which is a little village not far from Bristol, has chosen the next record in our programme.
i   Aunt Harriet used to sing quite well when she was a girl.
j   I licked the stamp, stuck it on the envelope, and then went out to post the letter.
k   He looked very surprised when he found that he had been sitting on a plate of sandwiches.
l   'I don't think a fox killed my chickens, Officer. I think my neighbour's dogs killed them.'
m   James Hill directed another film about animals.
n   Tiny sea creatures make coral.
o   My brother collects stamps.

4 It is clear from the first paragraph that a *cub* (*l*. 5) is a young fox, and that a *pup* (*l*. 10) – sometimes called a *puppy* – is a young dog.

In this exercise, find the animals in the second column that correspond with the young animals in the first column.

a   fawn   frog
b   lamb   swan
c   foal   deer
d   cub   sheep
e   kid   bear
f   chick   goat
g   calf   cow
h   kitten   horse
i   cygnet   hen
j   tadpole   cat

5 Write a very short account in not more than 40 words, of the story of the film 'The Belstone Fox'.

6

Clues across

1 A place with mineral water springs; often a holiday resort (3)
5 Abbreviation for laboratory (3)
7 A person who is unable to walk properly (7)
9 Suitable; fitting (3)
11 Beer (3)
12 Domestic animal (3)
14 Machine for printing (5)
16 Ale (4)
18 Journey (4)
20 Shaw's play about a famous Frenchwoman (5,4)
21 The lowest point; nothing (4)
22 When I have to remember something important, I tie a _____ in my handkerchief (4)
23 A kind of gun (5)
26 Of it, or it is (3)
28 Verb: to take legal action against (3)
29 Verb: to request (3)
31 Little balls (7)
32 Used to lock, or unlock, a door (3)
33 Used to fasten two things (perhaps pieces of cloth or paper) together (3)

Clues down

1 A lot of salt water; (there is a black one, a red one and a yellow one!) (3)
2 Verb: to do (3)
3 Someone who does not tell the truth (4)
4 Monkeys (4)
5 Past of lead (3)
6 Very wet, swampy ground (3)
8 Abundant (9)
10 Gift (7)
13 Threatening; something terrible is going to happen (7)
14 Previous (5)
15 Verb: to put fuel on a fire (5)
17 Something to hear with (3)
19 Past of run (3)
24 Island (4)
25 Vegetable like an onion (4)
26 Liquid to write with (3)
27 Secret agent (3)
29 A kind of small snake (Cleopatra was killed by one) (3)
30 Relatives; people of the same family (3)

17

'New Swiss Guards enrolled at Vatican ceremony'

VATICAN CITY, May 7 (AP) -- Fourteen Swiss Guards and a new commander were sworn in yesterday in a colorful ceremony on the anniversary of the massacre of 147 members of the Vatican Army in 1527.

5 The recruits bring up the corps to 70 men, the greatest number since the death of Pope John XXIII in 1963.

Dressed in the blue, red and yellow parade uniform designed by Michelangelo, the guards marched to St. Damasus' courtyard to the roll of drums. They then swore to protect the Pope and his suc-

10 cessors with their lives.

Earlier the guards attended a Mass in the Church of St. Martin celebrated by Msgr. Giovanni Benelli, the Vatican's under-secretary of state. They also paid tribute to the monument to the guards who died in St. Peter's Square in 1527 while defending

15 Pope Clement VII during the sack of Rome by the troops of Charles V.

The guards are recruited in Switzerland and must be 25 years old, Catholic and unmarried. Since the death of Pope John XXIII, when the force was cut to 110 men, the corps has steadily dwin-

20 dled. In 1972 it numbered only 51.

Low pay has reportedly brought on a number of resignations and has made it difficult for the Vatican to find recruits.

Pope Paul raised their pay and Social Security benefits in 1971 and the Vatican has stepped up recruiting efforts in Switzerland to

25 attract volunteers.

The new commander of the Swiss Guards is Pfyffer Von Altishofen. He had been serving as acting commander after his predecessor retired because of poor health.

sack (*l.* 15) destruction

dwindled (*l.* 19–20) got smaller and smaller

stepped up (*l.* 24) increased

1 Read the news item carefully, and then choose the best answers in the following exercise.

a What is the function of the Swiss Guard?

  a To attract volunteers from Switzerland.
  b To be 25 years old, Catholic, Swiss and unmarried.
  c To protect the Pope.

b Who might become a member of the Swiss guard?

  a Somebody not more than 25 and a Catholic.
  b A Swiss Catholic bachelor, at least 25 years old.
  c A 25-year-old Catholic living in Switzerland.

c When was the Swiss Guard at its smallest number?

  a On the death of Pope John XXIII.
  b In 1972.
  c In 1963.

d Why are there more Swiss guards now?

  a Because the pay and conditions are better.
  b Because some new ones were sworn in on May 7th.
  c Because they are necessary to defend the Pope.

e Why did the previous commander of the Swiss Guards retire?

  a Because he did not earn enough money.
  b Because he was too old to continue.
  c Because he was ill.

2 Answer the following questions, basing your answers on the information in the passage.

a What happened in 1963?
b What happened on 7th May, 1527?
c What had happened by 1972?
d What happens in Switzerland?
e What happened in 1971?
f What happened on 7th May, 1973?
g What happened before the ceremony?
h What has happened to attract more recruits?
i What has been happening since 1963?
j What happens when a new Swiss Guard takes the oath?

Now, here are ten answers. Still using information in the passage, write ten questions to which these might be the answers.

Example: Three. (Question: How many fingers are raised in the traditional salute?)

k 110 men
l in the church of St. Martin
m Michelangelo

n fourteen
o Clement VII
p red, blue and yellow

q	the new commander of the Swiss Guards	s	because they were not very well paid
r	to protect the Pope	t	in St. Peter's Square

3 . . . the guards who died in St. Peter's Square *in* 1527 *while* defending Pope Clement VII *during* the sack of Rome. (*l.* 13–15)

From the following list, fill in the spaces in these sentences with an appropriate word

> on   at   during   in   while   about   after
> before   for   by   since

a   We were awoken _____ three o'clock by a loud bang.

b   _____ you were out, several people telephoned.

c   Where were you _____ the first three months of last year?

d   I was born _____ two o'clock _____ the afternoon, _____ 22nd July, 1941.

e   She is very lazy and never gets up _____ nine o'clock. Her husband, on the other hand, is always in his office _____ eight o'clock _____ the latest.

f   _____ we came to this town, we lived in Exton _____ five years, and _____ we were there our two youngest children were born.

g   I don't know exactly, but it must have been _____ midnight when I heard the noise, because I got home _____ half past eleven, and I had been in the house _____ half an hour. It happened _____ I was brushing my teeth, I remember, just _____ going to bed.

h   _____ I had waited _____ ten minutes (_____ which time several people passed through the office), a girl put her head round the door and told me that Mr Grey just had time to see me _____ ten minutes _____ he went for his lunch.

i   It has been a most eventful year so far. _____ February my mother-in-law died, _____ being very ill for several months. My wife was very depressed _____ her mother's death, and I sent her to the sea-side _____ a couple of weeks. _____ her holiday, she met an old friend, quite by chance, whom she hadn't seen _____ they were at school together. _____ May 10th my wife and I celebrated our Silver Wedding, and _____ the same day our daughter Patricia got engaged; she hopes to get married _____ the autumn. We are having a new house built. It has been under construction _____ nearly two years, but we hope to have moved in _____ Christmas.

j   The wedding will take place _____ 23rd May _____ ten o'clock _____ the morning.

4 The guards *marched* to St. Damasus' Courtyard. (*l.* 8) Look at these ten verbs. They are all verbs of movement. Put each verb, in its appropriate form, into one of the spaces in the following sentences.

> jump   fly   stagger   sprint   hop   slip
> wade   shuffle   limp   toddle

a The runners ——— to the finishing-post.

b I could tell he was drunk because he was ——— from one side of the road to the other.

c The baby ——— across the room towards his mother.

d I'll be back in a moment. I must just ——— down to the shop for some sugar.

e The poor old man ——— down the road.

f She had hurt her ankle, and ——— painfully into the room.

g There was no bridge, but luckily the river was not deep and we were able to ——— across.

h Ten people were trapped in the burning building, and they ——— into blankets held by firemen in the street below.

i When she heard the postman arrive, she ——— down the stairs as she was expecting a letter from her fiancé.

j He could only find one shoe, so he ——— across the room on one foot.

5 This is an account of a 'colourful ceremony'. Write a similar account of a colourful ceremony you have seen, in about 300 words. (The story, as printed, is about 300 words.)

or

Rewrite this story, as if for a second edition of the newspaper, in not more than 100 words.

6 This strip has no words, but the story is quite clear from the pictures. Write the story, in a short paragraph, in your own words. Begin like this: Every summer, George and Gaye . . .

18

SUNK! A QE2 holiday for 99 old folk

DAILY MIRROR
Friday,
September 29, 1972

NINETY-NINE old-age pension- ers will be told today that the holiday they booked a year ago is off.

The pensioners, who have each 5 paid £150·50 for an eleven-day cruise aboard the QE2, were due to sail from Southampton next Monday.

The liner will sail to New York on schedule without the pensioners be- 10 cause, for some reason, the Cunard computer failed to book them on the voyage.

Their holiday had been arranged by Mr Alan Doyle, a director of Saga 15 Senior Citizens Holidays, Folkestone —on September 30 last year.

Tickets

Mr Doyle said last night that the bookings were confirmed in Novem- 20 ber. A £2,000 booking fee was paid in January, the balance of £13,000 was paid last week—and passage tickets and travel documents were received by return post. 25

Mr Doyle said: 'Then this after- noon Cunard telephoned me and said the voyage was off.'

Last night Cunard were sending telegrams to the 99 pensioners offer- 30 ing them an alternative holiday.

A company spokesman said: 'We are offering them a BOAC flight to New York, hotels for four nights, all meals, all sightseeing trips including 35 one to Washington, then the return trip to Southampton in QE2.'

Frightened

He added: 'If they don't want to fly then we will have to try to find some 40 other alternative.'

Mr Doyle said: 'Many of the pen- sioners are too frightened to fly. That's why they wanted to go both ways on the QE2.' 45

One of the pensioners, Mrs Dorothy Broadbent, of Chingford, Essex, said last night: 'We had been looking forward to this as a once-in-a-life- time holiday.' 50

QE2 (headline) Queen Elizabeth the Second, the great ocean liner belonging to the Cunard company

old-age pensioners (l. 1–2) men over 65 and women over 60 years of age

Senior Citizens (l. 16) a more diplomatic way of saying 'old-age pensioners'

1

In this story, very many different tenses are used.

The liner *will sail* to New York on schedule. (*l.* 9–10)
The Cunard booking computer *failed* to book them on the voyage.
(*l.* 16–17)
Their holiday *had been arranged* by Mr Alan Doyle. (*l.* 19–20)
The bookings *were confirmed* in November. (*l.* 26–27)
Last night Cunard *were sending* telegrams. (*l.* 39–40)
'*We are offering* them a BOAC flight to New York.' (*l.* 44–45)
'*We had been looking forward* to this.' (*l.* 66–67)

Now put the verbs in these sentences into their right tenses.

a I always (*break*) something when I (*wash*) up. Last week, I (*drop*)
three cups, and my wife (*be*) very angry. At the moment, she (*wash*)
up in the kitchen. She (*tell*) me not to help her any more.

b I (*read*) nearly all Hemingway's novels. Last week, I (*start*) to
read 'For Whom the Bell Tolls' and I nearly (*finish*) it now.
When I (*be*) in hospital last year I (*read*) 'A Farewell to Arms'.
When I (*finish*) 'For Whom the Bell Tolls' I (*start*) 'The Old Man
and the Sea'.

c Uncle Thomas (*go*) fishing every weekend, but he never (*catch*)
anything. His wife sometimes (*go*) with him, but she (*stay*) at
home last Saturday, because she (*catch*) a very bad cold and the
doctor (*tell*) her to stay in bed.

d I'm sorry, you can't see Mr Pritchard because he just (*go*) out. He
(*leave*) the office about three minutes ago, because he (*finish*) all
his work, and he (*not come*) back until tomorrow morning.

e She (*wear*) woollen pyjamas in the winter because she (*feel*) cold,
but her husband (*complain*) that she (*not look*) very glamorous.

f I (*wait*) here in the rain for a bus for nearly twenty minutes. It
(*rain*) every time I (*go*) out. I (*go*) to the Zoo last week, and as I
(*walk*) past the monkey-house it (*start*) to rain. I (*go*) inside to
shelter, but after I (*be*) there for ten minutes, I (*come*) out again
because the smell (*be*) so strong.

g I must write to my father to ask for some more money, as I (*spend*)
all mine. He always (*send*) me a cheque for my birthday, but I
(*have*) a lot of bills to pay since the beginning of the year, so I can't
wait for my birthday, which (*be*) in March.

h Doctor, please come quickly! My husband (*lie*) on the bathroom
floor. He (*make*) a very strange noise, his feet (*shake*) and his
knees (*knock*) together. I (*think*) he still (*breathe*) but I am not
sure.

2 Then this afternoon Cunard telephoned me and said the voyage was *off.* (*l.* 26–28)

Off can be used with other words to give many different meanings. Here are ten sentences using an idiomatic construction with *off.* Choose the best ending for each sentence.

a   The meat has gone off: never come near my house again.

b   We had to call off our trip to   I hope she has a good trip.
   France   because she and I don't hit it off.

c   Mary is off to Scotland   you should have put it in the
   tomorrow;   fridge.

d   I have been feeling off colour   because we didn't have enough
   lately;   money.

e   I always go out when my   and let me off with a warning.
   mother-in-law comes to   I think I'd better go to the
   visit us   doctor's.

f   Will you come to the station   to see me off.

g   Be off with you:

h   The policeman was very kind

3 Many of the pensioners are *too frightened to fly.* (*l.* 42–43) This means that many of the pensioners are so frightened that they will not fly.
Rewrite these sentences, using the same construction with *too.*

a   This coffee is so hot that nobody can drink it.
b   The little girl was so terrified that she was unable to speak.
c   Aunt Fanny is so fat that it is quite impossible for her to go through the door.
d   This news is so good that it cannot be true.
e   That ring is so cheap that it just cannot be gold.
f   Uncle Moses is so mean that he will never buy his wife a new dress.
g   I can't lift that box because it is so heavy.
h   I can't wear those trousers any more because they are so tight.
i   Those shoes are so good that it would be a pity to throw them away.
j   She speaks so quickly that I cannot understand her.

4 The *Daily Mirror* likes to use rather dramatic headlines – SUNK! A QE2 HOLIDAY FOR 99 OLD FOLK. State, in a few words, what you think each of the following headlines means.

a   BIG BANG SHATTERS WINDOWS
b   ELIZABETH'S NECKLINE BRINGS IN THE CUSTOMERS

c MIDNIGHT MADNESS AND MUSIC MAKERS
d WHOOSH! THERE GOES CONCORDE!
e PETER'S PINK PANTS: RED FACES AT WIMBLEDON

5 The story is written in about 270 words. Rewrite it for a later edition of the paper, keeping all the information that is necessary, in not more than 100 words.

6 Mrs Broadbent said that she had been looking forward to her trip in the QE2 as a 'Once-in-a-lifetime' holiday. Imagine that you have plenty of money at your disposal, and three months' holiday from your work. Describe, in about 300 words, what your 'once-in-a-lifetime holiday' would be like.

7

Clues across

1 Total (3)
5 A period of time (3)
7 A very useful thing to have if there are smokers in the house (7)
8 British Broadcasting Corporation (3)
10 A snake-like fish (3)
12 Used for sweetening (5)
14 Verb: to go up a mountain or up the stairs (5)
15 Mickey _____ (5)
16 Something to eat but not a full meal (5)
18 Not a liability, but something of value (5)

19 There are many varieties of this, (carving, pen, pocket, etc.), all used for cutting (5)
20 The housewife uses it to fasten her washing on the clothes line (3)
22 Conjunction (3)
24 The sport of shooting at a target with a bow and arrows (7)
25 'Every _____ has his day' (3)
26 Finish (3)

Clues down

1 Verb: to cry bitterly (3)
2 Short word meaning 'raincoat' (3)
3 A little bush in the garden (5)
4 Butter is made from this (5)
5 You have two but a needle has one! (3)
6 Everybody (3)
9 You must be careful not to lose your _____ or you will fall (7)
11 Oriental (7)
12 Verb: to hit with the palm of the hand (5)
13 Verb: to waken (5)
17 If there is no door-bell, you must _____ (5)
18 Not before (5)
20 'As like as two peas in a _____' (3)
21 Something put in the mouth to prevent someone from speaking (3)
22 The sailor says this word twice to mean 'yes' (3)
23 Past form of 'do' (3)

19

His heart stays in San Francisco

DAILY EXPRESS
Monday,
March 26, 1973

Sound 73
by David Wigg

TONY BENNETT, the American singer with the sophisticated following, currently touring Britain, can't remember how many times he has sung his standard hit "I Left My Heart In San Francisco."

He sang it again for the umpteenth time to his audience at the London Palladium, last night.

"I never get tired of singing it," he said. "I like it too much. It's a great city and it's a good song."

Recordings

Bennett is to record a TV special with American singer Lena Horne while he is here. And a new LP recorded by him in London for Philips entitled "Listen Easy" will be released in June.

"I like it here," he added quietly over champagne. "I would like to live here so many months of the year."

He already keeps a large flat in Grosvenor Square, where he is staying with his actress wife Sandie Grant and their three-year-old daughter Joanna. It has a studio where he likes to paint.

Tony plans to have his first exhibition later in the year and he has already sold one picture for £4,000.

At the end of the year Tony is to star in a musical film which has been specially written for him called "Two Bits," a slang expression for 50 cents.

It's about an Italian immigrant who goes to America, but he becomes a failure.

"In many ways it's very close to my life the way the story has been written," said Bennett. "My father, an Italian, was ill and died when I was nine. He always wanted me to sing, but he never lived long enough to be a part of my success."

The film is to be made by Italy's top director Vittoria De Sica.

---

standard hit (*l.* 7) a song that is always popular

umpteenth (*l.* 10) he has sung it so many times that nobody can say how many times he has sung it (not *six*teen or *eigh*teen, but *ump*teen!)

LP (*l.* 21) Long Playing record

1 Read the item carefully. Then choose the best answers in the following exercise.

a When Tony Bennett was interviewed by David Wigg, he was

    a recording a TV show.
    b making a musical film.
    c drinking champagne.

b Tony Bennett has sung 'I Left my Heart in San Francisco'

    a more times than he can remember.
    b eighteen or nineteen times.
    c so many times that he is tired of it.

c Tony Bennett wants to

    a buy a house and live in England.
    b live part of each year in England.
    c leave America and settle in England.

d Tony Bennett's hobby is

    a singing.
    b painting.
    c drinking champagne.

e Tony Bennett's father

    a was born in Italy and died in America.
    b liked his son's singing.
    c was glad that his son became famous.

2 Tony Bennett sang to his *audience* at the *London Palladium.* (l. 9–11) The *London Palladium* is a theatre, and *audience* is the word used for a lot of people in a theatre. Find similar words to fill the spaces in these sentences.

a The _____ played very badly, and lost the match.
b The train had to go slowly, because a _____ of workmen were working on the line.
c Johnny worked very hard all the term, and was top of his _____ in the examinations.
d When the last passenger had left the ship, the _____ began to prepare for the next trip.
e There was such a large _____ that the church was not big enough to hold them all.
f The agency has expanded during the last year, and now we have a _____ of over thirty.
g The play has a very large _____; over twenty characters, in fact.
h A large _____ stood silently in front of the palace gates, waiting for news.
i His old _____, the Sixteenth Hussars, was disbanded and he was transferred to another one.

j The angry _____ threw stones and shouted insults, and the police had great difficulty in preventing serious damage.

3 He can't remember how many times he *has sung* the song. He *sang* it last night. (*l.* 5–12) Put the verbs in these sentences into the past or the present perfect.

a Charles Dickens (*write*) a lot of famous novels.
b I'm sorry, you can't speak to Mr Price. He just (*go*) out.
c Aunt Clarabella is in hospital because she (*break*) her leg.
d She (*shoot*) three tigers in India last year.
e Help! Come quickly! The baby (*swallow*) a button.
f I (*make*) a cake. Would you like a piece?
g 'You (*meet*) Miss Jones?' 'Yes, we (*meet*) at Jenny's party last week.'
h Open the door for me, please; I (*lose*) my key.
i No, you can't have any more money! I (*give*) you enough!
j She (*work*) in a fish shop before her marriage.

4 Tony Bennett has a *flat* in Grosvenor Square. (*l.* 29–30) Every day there are advertisements in the daily papers for flats and houses, but they are often hard to understand because so many abbreviations are used, for the sake of economy. Can you understand these?

a Norwood. 3 bedrm. furn. house, C.H., gge., 1 yr. or more, £30 p.w.
b Newly furn. lux. flat., 2 lge. dble. beds., 1 single, large kit., mod. bathrm., sep. W.C. Long let £50 p.w. Tel 743 7869 after 6 pm.
c Small cntry. cott., 2 beds., lge. sitt/dng. rm., mod. kit & bathrm. Lge. gdn., gge. £8,000 o.n.o.
d 30 mins. Cent. London. Mod. bung., 3 beds., mod. kit., dble. gge., near stn. Offers over £15,000.
e Nr. Bradford. Vict. det. hse., 5 beds, gdn. with car space, convt. stn. & buses. Unf. £25 p.w.

5 Tony plans to have his first exhibition later *in* the year and he has already sold one picture *for* £4,000. (*l.* 36–39) *In* and *for* are prepositions. Put in the appropriate prepositions in the following passages. Choose them from this list:

in, over, out, down, on, into, up, at, of, with, near, to, for, back, away, about, by, from, off.

a Cousin Anastasia went _____ _____ her bicycle yesterday afternoon. She had a bright red scarf tied _____ her head, to prevent the wind blowing her hair _____. Unluckily, Mr Brown's big bull caught sight _____ her as she was pedalling _____ the hill. Attracted _____ the red scarf, he charged _____ her and tossed her _____ the air. Poor Anastasia flew _____ the hedge and landed _____ the middle _____ the duck pond. She managed to get _____, but she was covered _____ head _____ foot _____ black mud.

b I am very angry _____ the local council. I left my car _____ the street _____ my flat while I went _____ the south _____ France _____ a week's holiday. When I came _____, the car was gone. The council workmen thought someone wanted to get rid _____ it, so they had taken it _____ the yard where all abandoned cars are sent. When I went _____ the yard to ask if I could have my car _____, it had already been put _____ a special machine which had compressed it. They gave it _____ me _____ a small cardboard box.

c Bill Adams pulled a nylon stocking _____ his head and went _____ to rob a jeweller's shop. He broke _____ the shop quite easily, without setting _____ the burglar alarm. Unfortunately, he forgot all _____ the stocking _____ his head, and when he happened to catch sight _____ himself _____ a mirror _____ chance, he was so frightened that he nearly jumped _____ _____ his skin. He screamed _____ the top _____ his voice, and woke _____ a policeman who was having a little sleep _____ a dark doorway nearby. I am going _____ visit Bill _____ Brixton Prison next Tuesday afternoon.

6 The item about Tony Bennett is about 280 words long. Rewrite it, for a later edition of the newspaper, in not more than 100 words.

7 Tell the story in your own words. Begin: When Gaye's friend Polly came to visit her . . .

20

THE TIMES
Saturday, June 30, 1973

Five feared lost after sinking of Scots ship

From Ronald Faux
Glasgow, June 29

Five men are feared lost after the Clyde coaster Glen Shiel, 240 tons, sank early today off the coast of Ayrshire.
5 A search by lifeboat and helicopter was launched after one of the crew, Mr James Scott, aged 21, of Portrush, Northern Ireland, staggered ashore on
10 rocks at Troon. He had spent seven hours in the water and was taken to hospital with exposure and shock.

The Glen Shiel belonged to
15 the Glen light shipping company of Glasgow and was sailing from Ayr to Glasgow and Portree, in the Isle of Skye.

The missing men are Mr
20 Thomas West, ship's master, of Gordonstoun, Mr Thomas Farquhar, engineer, of Port Gordon, both Banff, Mr James Feirman, engineer, of Dunoon,
25 Mr John McInnes, mate, of Glasgow and Mr Gordon Davies, a passenger.

Mr Scott told the police that two and a half miles out from
30 Ayr the ship began to list and heeled over. He jumped from the side and saw two other men diving into the water. The vessel went down almost
35 immediately.

Shortly after he scrambled ashore, wreckage from the Glen Shiel was seen drifting on to the rocks. Later a fishing boat reported bubbles of oil in the 40 area.

Royal Navy divers were standing by and a naval rescue helicopter, lifeboats and shipping which had answered an 45 emergency call, were searching for survivors around Lady Isle.

There was no sign of the missing men and a Royal Navy officer said the chances of 50 anyone else being found alive were slim.

The weather at the time was described by the Glasgow weather centre as "reason- 55 able", with no more than fresh winds.

to list (l. 30) to lean over to one side

to heel over (l. 31) has the same meaning (both these verbs are only used for ships)

1 Read the news story carefully, and then give *short* answers to these questions.

a How many men were on the 'Glen Shiel'?
b Were there any passengers on the boat?
c How long was Mr Scott in the water?
d Where was the 'Glen Shiel' going?
e What is a 'coaster'?
f Why was Mr Scott taken to hospital?
g How soon did the boat sink after she started to lean over?
h Who saw bubbles of oil in the area?
i What is the opinion of the Royal Navy officer about the missing men?
j Was the weather bad at the time?

Using only information from the story, write questions to which these phrases might be the answers. For example *21* might be the answer to the question 'How old is James Scott?'.

k near Ayrshire
l 'Glen Shiel'
m lifeboats and a helicopter
n the Glen light shipping company of Glasgow
o because the ship had begun to sink
p no, he swam ashore
q yes, it was seen drifting on to the rocks
r none
s it is very unlikely
t fresh

2 Mr James Scott *staggered* ashore on rocks at Troon. (*l.* 7–10) Look at these ten verbs, which have certain similarities in meaning, and at the ten sentences that follow them. Put each verb, in a suitable form, into its most appropriate sentence.

> stroll   rush   mince   swagger   jolt   stride
> hobble   totter   inch   ooze

a There was a stone in my shoe, and I _____ painfully towards the seat.
b All the children _____ joyfully out of the classroom the moment the bell rang.
c The road was very rough and the cart _____ over the stones.
d Oil was _____ slowly from a small hole in the side of the can.
e The policeman _____ his way slowly along the ledge to where the boy was hanging by his finger-tips.
f Her shoes had very high heels and her skirt was so tight that she _____ down the street in a ridiculously affected manner.
g Joe was very proud of having won the fight, and he _____ out of the ring in the direction of the dressing room.

85

h Without hesitation, the officer _____ purposefully towards the angry crowd.

i The poor old man could hardly stand but with the aid of two sticks he _____ uncertainly towards us.

j John and Elizabeth _____ hand in hand beside the river.

3 *Five* rhymes with *alive* but not with *give*. *Good* rhymes with *would* but not with *food*.

Here are five words from the news story. Underline the words in the groups that follow that rhyme with the main word.

Coast (*l.* 4)   nosed   post   toast   lost   roast   most
                  cost   boast   host   ghost

Search (*l.* 5) church   perch   arch   urge   birch   harsh
                  marsh   shirts torch

Call (*l.* 45)   tall   ball   haul   pal   brawl   snarl
                  stall   crawl   tail   foul

Isle (*l.* 46)   mile   dial   oil   male   nail   style
                  while   pile   pill   I'll

Found (*l.* 50) drowned round   pound   hound   frowned
                  mount   warned browned owned

4 The vessel *went down* almost immediately (*l.* 32–35) is another way of saying that the vessel *sank* almost immediately.

Rewrite these sentences, replacing the expressions *in italics* by a phrasal verb (a verb with a preposition, like *go down* in place of *sink*), and making any other changes that may be necessary.

a Uncle Ben *arrived unexpectedly* last weekend.
b The police are *investigating* the matter carefully.
c My opponent *surrendered* after the first round of the fight.
d Don't *abandon* hope – she may *telephone* later.
e Jim and Julia have *terminated* their engagement.
f I managed to *persuade* her to lend me her car.
g They have *refused to accept* my offer of £18,000 for the house.
h The car *gradually stopped* in front of the theatre.
i The maid managed to *extinguish* the fire without calling the fire brigade.
j The numbers of students have been *decreasing* lately.

5 *Wreckage was seen drifting onto the rocks* (*l.* 37–39) is another way of saying that somebody saw wreckage which was drifting onto the rocks.

Rewrite these sentences in the same way.

a Somebody heard a nightingale which was singing in the forest.
b They noticed a large bundle of banknotes which was lying in the road.
c They saw a wounded man who was staggering up the hill.
d Somebody spotted a body which was floating near the coast.

e They observed a strange object which was flying over the sea.

f They heard a bell which was ringing in the next room.

g They heard a strange noise which was coming from under the bed.

h Somebody noticed three men who were swimming towards the shore.

i Somebody noted an unpleasant smell coming from the cellar.

j They watched two middle-aged women who were leaving the building with a heavy bag.

6 The story as it is printed is about 275 words long. Rewrite it, for a second edition of the newspaper, in not more than 90 words.

7 Imagine that you are Mr James Scott. Tell the story in your own words.

8

Clues across

6 Important industrial city in the north of England (9)

7 A kind of small, plain cake, often made in Scotland (5)

9 A musical instrument (5)

11 All right! (2)

12 A king who is no longer a king is called an _____ king (2)

13 One of Shakespeare's greatest tragedies (7)

14 'As You Like _____' is one of Shakespeare's comedies (2)

16 Infinitive form of the verb 'I am' (2)

17 Less wet (5)

19 Verb: to sing in a strange and special way, as they do in the Alps (5)

22 A very large and important church (9)

Clues down

1 Opposite of white (5)

2 In which bread is baked (4)

3 The ship that Noah built (3)

4 A hammer, or a saw, or a spanner, for example (4)

5 Kind of stone often used for making roofs (5)

7 Not liquid (5)

8 Sometimes used as an anaesthetic (5)

9 Foolishness (5)

10 Verb: to send away (5)

15 Verb: to find something or someone by inquiries. Or noun: a sign of something that formerly existed (5)

16 They ring! (5)

18 I have three meals a day, but my wife _____ only twice (4)

20 Two of these are usually necessary for rowing a boat (4)

21 You sleep in it! (3)

Gas 'won't kill mouse

But five hours later 21 people died in blast

GAS board men looking for a leak told a shop girl there was 'not enough gas to kill a
5 **mouse.'**

Less than five hours later the shopping precinct, in which 21 people died, lay in ruins from an explosion, the
10 blast inquiry was told yesterday.

Miss Catherine Proctor, 18, told the inquiry at Paisley, Renfrewshire, that she was
15 given the assurance after she complained of smelling gas in the display window of the clothes shop w h e r e she worked.

20 She is one of the survivors of the blast at Clarkston Toll, near Glasgow, last October. More than 100 people were injured.

25 Her boss, Mr Hamish Robertson, 30, said that on the day of the explosion he rang the gas board for an inspector or supervisor after
30 learning that the men digging the road outside were sub-contractors.

Witnesses told of smelling gas three weeks before the
35 explosion and said they were concerned that the gas board workmen were using pneumatic drills and a butane gas burner.

40 Mrs Ivy McAdam, 46, manageress of a furniture shop blown up, said she asked one of the workmen who was using a drill on the pavement outside
45 the shop if he could play a bugle and added : 'Well, you want to learn because you will be joining Gabriel when you're in the gas pipe.' The work-
50 men laughed.

The explosion came like a flash of blue lightning. Her boss, Mr Sidney Dalziell, 66, was 'lifted like a little puppet and he went with the filing 55 cabinet.'

She held on to Mr Dalziell's hand until they were both rescued.

Police Inspector John Mac- 60 Donald told the inquiry he was concerned about the 'very strong' smell of gas on the morning of the day of the explosion. He asked the gas 65 board superintendent if he wanted anything done about people in the shops or the street. He was told there was 70 no danger.

Inspector MacDonald said he did not use the word 'evacuation' but that was in his mind. He also felt that 75 some sort of warning about smoking could have been given.

The inquiry continues today.

1 Read the news item carefully, and then choose the best answers in this exercise.

a The men from the Gas Board told the girl

    a they could not find any gas leaking.
    b there was some gas leaking but they could not find out where.
    c there was very little gas leaking.

b Mr Robertson telephoned the Gas Board because

    a he could smell gas.
    b he wanted an inspector to come to his shop and look for a gas leak.
    c the men digging outside his shop were not from the Gas Board.

c The witnesses at the inquiry said that they had been worried because

    a Gas Board men were digging holes in the street.
    b so many holes had been dug in the street.
    c dangerous equipment was being used.

d Mrs McAdam and Mr Dalziell were

    a both thrown through the air by the explosion.
    b injured in the explosion, but not seriously.
    c trapped in their shop by the explosion.

e Police Inspector John MacDonald asked the Gas Board superintendent

    a if the police should take any measures to protect the people.
    b if gas was escaping from the pipe in front of the shops or not.
    c if gas was escaping inside the shops or outside in the street.

2 More than 100 people were *injured*. (*l*. 23–24) Look at these ten words, which have certain similarities in meaning, and at the sentences that follow. Put each word (in its appropriate form) into its right sentence.

    injure   hurt   wound   pain   ache   bleed
    damage   harm   sting   suffer

a After the battle, the dead were buried and the _____ were taken to hospital.

b I have cut myself with this stupid new razor; what can I put on to stop the _____ ?

c He ate twenty-five ripe peaches; it isn't surprising that he had a _____ in his stomach.

d This antiseptic may _____ a little when I put it on, but it will do you good.

e 'Why are you crying, little girl?' 'Because I fell down and _____ my knee.'

f The poor man died after _____ for many years from an incurable disease.

g I shouldn't have walked so far yesterday; my legs _____ terribly this morning.

h Smoking too much often _____ the lungs and the respiratory system.

i Sixteen people were fatally _____ in the train smash.

j Irreparable _____ was done to the brain tissue.

3 The Gas Board men were *looking for* a leak. (*l*. 1–2) The verb *look* may be used with many different prepositions to give different meanings. Fill the spaces in these sentences.

a She is very vain. She is always looking _____ herself in the mirror.

b I have forgotten his telephone number. I must look it _____ in the directory.

c They were very proud, snobbish people, and always looked _____ on their poorer relations.

d This is the third time that washing has been stolen from the line in my back garden: I must ask the police to look _____ it.

e Look _____ your work carefully before you give it to the teacher for correction.

f The wall was quite high, so she stood on a box to look _____.

g Take your raincoat with you to the football match; it looks _____ rain.

h Are you looking _____ _____ your trip to Argentina?

4 Mrs Ivy McAdam is the manageress of a *furniture shop*. (*l*. 40–41) But shops are often given the name, in the possessive form, of the man whose business is carried on there. For example, a *baker*'s is 'a shop of a baker', at which you could buy bread. Write down the names of two things that you would be able to buy at each of the following shops.

a butcher's	**d** florist's	**g** draper's
b greengrocer's	**e** ironmonger's	**h** fishmonger's
c stationer's	**f** chemist's	**i** grocer's

And if you were shopping in a big department store, what two things could you buy in each of these departments?

a soft furnishings	**f** fancy goods
b gentlemen's outfitting	**g** hardware
c delicatessen	**h** hosiery
d haberdashery	**i** household lines
e dress fabrics	**j** millinery

An *electrician* would come to your house to do any electrical repairs that were necessary, or you might employ a *gardener* to work in your garden. What work do these people do?

a plumber	**d** charwoman	**g** paperhanger
b glazier	**e** chimney-sweep	**h** dustman
c nanny	**f** decorator	**i** barber

5 The story has a headline – GAS 'WON'T KILL MOUSE' – followed by a subsidiary one – BUT FIVE HOURS LATER 21 PEOPLE DIED IN BLAST. Write, in not more than a few words, what sort of story you would expect to find under the following headlines.

    a ACTRESS TO MARRY OIL MILLIONAIRE: 'IT'S REALLY LOVE THIS TIME'.

    b FINED FOR SPEEDING: 'SPEEDOMETER NOT WORKING' SAYS PROFESSOR.

    c CASTLE TO BE PULLED DOWN: 'TOO COSTLY TO REPAIR' SAYS COUNCIL.

    d 'NOWHERE TO SLEEP': STUDENT FINED FOR TRESPASSING IN MUSEUM.

    e SINGER TO RETIRE: 'WANT MORE TIME WITH THE CHILDREN'.

6 Newspaper reporter Jim Taylor went to a jeweller's shop after the police had been called in to investigate a robbery. Here are the notes that Jim made, before going back to his office to write the story. Write the story from these notes, in about 100 words.

Hutchinson's (jewellers). 8.30 a.m. (shop opens 9). Manager (Peter Bell, 42) already there. Two men (no description – very young?) in small car (possible Mini? Volkswagen?). Brick through window. Grabbed three trays of rings. (Diamonds.) Manager just put them there. Manager in strong room at time. Heard crash – rushed out – too late. Police arrived five minutes later. No description of men – no number of car (street practically deserted). Rings worth about £15,000.

7 Now make similar notes that you think the reporter may have made before writing the story in this section. Remember that the story is about the inquiry into the explosion in the Clarkston Toll shopping precinct, about three months after the event.

8 Flivver and Miggy (the Gambols' niece and nephew) spent the Christmas holidays with George and Gaye. One evening, they all went to the circus. Tell this story in your own words.

22

A

THE DAILY MAIL
May 10, 1973

He's got all the answers

FREE BOOKS!

He'll give you some free books to take home. If you're not sure where to find him, post the coupon.

Anything you might want to know, the life, the work, the prospects in the RAF. He can tell you about the pay, about the sort of people you'll be working with if you join. You can ask him anything. He'll give you a straight answer. He's at your nearest RAF Careers Information Office—address in phone book.

To:
RAF
Careers
(7.TZ.3),
Government
Buildings,
London Rd,
Stanmore,
Middlesex
HA7 4PZ.

Smart Girl

Name (Mr, Mrs or Miss)

Address

Date of birth

Royal Air Force

Formal application must be made in the UK

B

There aren't many jobs this secure

A career in the police is one of the steadiest jobs going. With plenty of chances to get on, interesting work, and a good pension at the end of it. And straight off you're on £1,251 basic (more in London). Plus free housing or a generous rent allowance.

If you are aged 19-30, 5′ 8″ or over and physically fit, send off this coupon today.

Send for brochure to Police Careers Officer, Home Office, Dept. J159. London SW1A 2AP

Name

Address

County

Age

Do a great job in Britain's POLICE

THE DAILY EXPRESS
May 8, 1973

C

Work in a job where you're needed every day.

You can be a State Enrolled Nurse (good general education, 2 years training).

Or a State Registered Nurse ('O' levels, 3 years training).

The work asks a lot of you but it's interesting and varied.

For 2 years you get 4 weeks holiday a year.

After that, 5 weeks a year.

For leaflets giving the full story post the coupon.

People remember nurses.

I may become a nurse. Please send me the facts.

NAME (Miss/Mrs/Mr)

ADDRESS

AGE

TO: The Chief Nursing Officer, Dept. of Health and Social Security, P.O. Box 702, London, SW20 8SZ. (in Scotland, write to The Chief Nursing Officer, St. Andrew's House, Edinburgh, EH1 3DE.)

RCG DE C1

THE DAILY EXPRESS
May 8, 1973

D

Britannia Airways

AIR STEWARDESSES

An adventurous, exciting career could be yours flying with us the holiday centres of Europe. Neat appearance, ability to de with people, aged between 20–30 with good educational bac ground. Foreign language and nursing/first aid qualificatio an advantage. Full-time employment for six months leading permanent appointments.

Based at Luton Airport.

Write for application form to:

Chief Stewardess
BRITANNIA AIRWAYS LTD.,
Luton Airport, Luton LU2 9ND, Beds.

1 Here are four advertisements, A, B, C & D. Which of the jobs described would be most suitable for the following people to apply for?

a Girl aged 21, at present working in an office. She has 'O' levels in English, mathematics, history and general science. She is short and rather fat. She is also rather shy, but very strong and not at all lazy.

b Young man aged 25. He has a good job in a chemical factory, but finds it rather boring. He prefers an out-of-door life. He is good-looking but not tall, very healthy and interested in sport.

c Boy of 18, studying for 'A' levels at school. He already has 'O' levels in five subjects, including French. Very keen on sport and not interested in working in an office. He wears glasses but is in very good physical condition.

d Girl of 22, at present working in a book-shop, but she doesn't like the job very much. She is very keen on sport (tennis and swimming). She has no plans for marriage, but wants a good job that will offer her security and interest.

e Woman of 28, divorced but with no children. She worked as a dentist's receptionist before her marriage. She is attractive and very smart. She has 4 'O' levels, and certificates of proficiency in typing and shorthand.

f Man of 27, married and with three children. He left school at 15, and since then has worked as a bus-driver. Very interested in football and boxing; he plays for his local team and has boxed as an amateur middle-weight.

g 20-year-old man, married but with no children. Working at present in a garage. He wants to see the world and to be sure of a steady job.

2 He's *got* all the answers. (*l.* 1: advertisement A) The verb *to get* is used very often in English, and has many different meanings. Rewrite these sentences, using the verb *to get*.

Example: I always rise at 6.30. I always *get up* at 6.30.

a I received a letter from my Aunt Charlotte yesterday.
b Peter has been ill but now he is recovering,
c My daughter was married six months ago.
d I was preparing to go to bed when somebody knocked at the door.
e They asked me to buy them some books that they could not obtain in their own town. (Two *gets* in this sentence, please!)
f There are plenty of chances to improve your position in the Police Force.
g They have a lot of books and their collection becomes bigger every year.

h For the first two years as a nurse, you are given four weeks holiday a year.

i She received a shock when she was told that she was going to have twins.

j I'm going to bed early because I have a headache.

3 Now, add the necessary prepositions in these sentences. They are all expressions using the verb *to get*.

a It took me a long time to get _____ my illness.

b She got _____ her scooter and rode away.

c I think I am going to be sick! Stop the bus! I want to get _____ !

d I don't understand what you are getting _____. Please explain it again.

e She managed to get _____ her parents to buy her a motor-cycle.

f Get _____ ! Get _____ ! They are firing at us!

g She got _____ her album and showed us the photographs of her grandchildren.

h I tried to phone my sister in Argentina, but I couldn't get _____ .

i Uncle Ebenezer has got rheumatism, and can't get _____ as well as he used to.

4 'I *may* become a nurse' (advertisement C) means 'It is quite possible and likely that I will become a nurse'. 'I *might* become a nurse' means that it is possible that I will become a nurse but it is not at all probable. *May I* _____? is also a way of asking permission to do something. Put *may* or *might* into the spaces in these sentences.

a She _____ be able to help you with your algebra homework, because she studied mathematics at the university.

b You are going to the South of France for your summer holiday? Take an umbrella! It _____ rain!

c We _____ buy a new car next year, but I'm afraid they are very expensive.

d _____ I have another cup of coffee, please?

e Don't put the car in the garage, dear. I _____ need it later.

f They _____ have written but we have received no letters for more than a week because of the postal strike.

g You _____ have told me that you had just polished the floor. I slipped. I _____ have injured myself seriously.

h He _____ arrive on the next train, but as it is already so late I don't think it is very likely.

5 He can tell you about the *pay* (advertisement A). Put the correct words into the spaces in these sentences.

Choose your words from this list

income	pay	wages	salary	grant	tip
ransom	fee	pension	deposit		

a The solicitor's _____ was very high but the advice he gave me was well worth all that money.

b He must have a huge _____ to live in the style he does, but he never seems to do any work.

c I earned nothing while I was a student but the Government gave me a generous _____.

d Don't forget to give the waiter a good _____ when we leave.

e Every Friday night when I get home I hand over my _____ to my wife.

f You can expect an annual increase in _____.

g After Aunt Emmeline retired from her job in the bank, she lived on her _____.

h The work is hard but the _____ is good.

i I paid £5 _____ and they said I could pay the rest at the end of the month.

j The kidnappers asked for a _____ of £100,000, all in used notes, for the safe return of Sir Jasper's daughter.

6

Clues across

6 An adjective with two meanings; a) not very important, b) neutral (11)

7 You may sit on it in a park or work at it in a factory (5)

9 Not precise (5)

10 Past tense of to hope (5)

11 A person who tries to find out military secrets and give them to an enemy (3)

12 What is left of your cigarette after you have smoked it (3)

13 A very sour fruit (5)

15 Danger (5)

16 A house that has been shut up for many years may have a _____ smell (5)

18 December 31st (3–5–3)

Clues down

1 If you study hard and learn to speak several languages you may become one (11)

2 To hurt someone by pressing his flesh between your finger and thumb. (Slang – to steal) (5)

3 Opposite of on (3)

4 Not narrow (5)

5 Nosy (11)

8 When on holiday, you may stay here (5)

9 Poison, especially that of a snake (5)

13 A country of North Africa (5)

14 She will look after you when you are ill (5)

17 In England, you can buy drinks here, but not if you are under 18 (3)

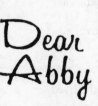

Dear Abby

By Abigail Van Buren
(© Chicago Tribune—N.Y. News Synd., Inc.)

DEAR ABBY: I can certainly feel for that widow with dentures who is worried about how men would feel about a woman if they knew she wore dentures.
5 I am 34, divorced, and just got mine. I am well-adjusted in other areas, but I dread meeting a fellow I might like, and then having to tell him I wear dentures.

Your advice to keep her mouth shut
10 won't help her much. If she becomes romantically involved with a man, I am sure they will do more than just hold hands, and he will surely learn the truth if they do any passionate kissing.

15 I hope you hear from men telling you how they feel about a woman with dentures because this is my problem, too.
'G' IN BROOKLYN

DEAR G.: My dental consultants
20 **assure me that dentures can be made so realistically that their presence will be undetected during the most passionate kissing. [Unless you get a kiss that will cause you to drop your**
25 **teeth, which is highly unlikely.] But please read on. . . .**

DEAR ABBY: In my 84 years I have never heard it suggested that a man's emotional responses to a woman might be
30 affected by her wearing dentures!

I refer to your column in the Columbus Citizen: If that woman signed 'Feeling Low' is concerned lest the man in whom she is interested would find her less attrac-
35 tive if he knew she wore dentures, she should put him to the test as soon as possible. If there is a remote chance that his attitude proves to be as she fears, the sooner she finds out what a jerk he is, the
40 better. Yours truly,
WARREN CHADBOURNE,
GROVE CITY, O.
DEAR WARREN: Your letter will bring joy to the hearts of many a lady
45 **who smiles thru her dentures. Thanks for writing.**

DEAR ABBY: That letter about dentures took me back to when I courted my second wife. She told me she had some-
50 thing to 'confess' before we married. Then she said, 'I wear false teeth, dear.'

I replied, 'That's all right, sweetheart. So do I.'

Then she smiled and said, 'Yours are
55 obvious, and before we're married I think you ought to fix yourself up with some that don't clack.' [P.S. I did.]
GRAMPS

DEAR ABBY: You told that widow
60 with dentures that the man who marries her should be glad he won't have any more dental bills to pay. Whooaa, girl!

Even tho her dentures may fit perfectly now, mechanical teeth do wear out. And
65 one's mouth and jaw formation changes, requiring new dentures. Theoretically dentures should be changed every five years—like an automobile, to adjust to muscle changes. And don't forget break-
70 age! 'DOC'

DEAR ABBY: Some lady wanted to know how men felt about women who wore false teeth. I have had lots of experience along that line as I am 80 years
75 old and have had five wives. [Four died and one divorced me.] The last four had false teeth when I married them and I didn't think a thing of it. I am going with a lady right now who has false teeth, and
80 it doesn't make any difference to me. I really think I prefer women with false teeth because they talk less.
'HAVE FALSIES [TEETH], TOO'

DEAR ABBY: Tell the gal who's sen-
85 sitive about her dentures not to worry. They won't keep the guys away.

I married one with china clippers and a padded bra because I thought all the rest of her was real. Too late I found out she
90 was also false-hearted. That blew it!
BILL IN TACOMA

---

dentures (*l.* 2) false teeth, artificial teeth

jerk (*l.* 39) a scoundrel; a dishonest or immoral person

thru (*l.* 45) (American spelling) through

clack (*l.* 57) to make a noise, such as two pieces of plastic striking together

whooaa! (*l.* 62) stop!

tho (*l.* 63) (American spelling) though

gal (*l.* 83) girl

guys (*l.* 85) men

china clippers (*l.* 86) false teeth

padded bra (*l.* 87) artificially enlarged brassière

that blew it! (*l.* 89) that finished it!

1 Read the letters and answers carefully, and then choose the best answers in the exercise.

a 'G' in Brooklyn has

    a always had false teeth.
    b a dread of wearing false teeth.
    c been wearing false teeth for a very short time.

b 'G' in Brooklyn wants

    a to know what men think about women with false teeth.
    b to talk about a problem that she has with her false teeth.
    c help with a problem that she has involving men.

c Warren Chadbourne tells the woman (who wrote a letter signed 'Feeling Low') that

    a she should not tell her man friend that she has false teeth.
    b women are less attractive if they wear dentures.
    c a man who is truly in love will not care if the woman has false teeth.

d 'Have Falsies (Teeth) Too' is an old man

    a whose wives all had false teeth.
    b who is not married at the moment.
    c who likes talkative women.

e Bill's wife

    a was sensitive about her dentures.
    b was not true to him.
    c had false teeth, but Bill didn't know until later.

2 *He will surely learn the truth if they do any passionate kissing.* (*l.* 13–14)

There are three types of conditional sentence, and this is an example of the first.

a Its formula is *future + if + present*, and it is used when it is *probable* that something will happen, with a certain result. Here it is suggested that he will *probably* kiss her passionately, and so definitely discover that she has false teeth.

b The second type of conditional sentence has the formula *conditional + if + past*. *He would surely learn the truth if they did any passionate kissing.* Here the event is not *likely* to take place, but it is *possible*. In other words, we do not expect that he will kiss her.

c The third type is *conditional perfect + if + past perfect*. The sentence in this case refers to something in the past and has no connection with the present at all. *He would surely have learned the truth if they had done any passionate kissing.* But they did not kiss passionately, and so he did not learn that her teeth were false.

Choose the correct endings for these ten sentences.

a	I would have told you	if I had a lot of money?
b	They will get a shock	if I had had toothache.
c	Uncle Max will come	if you pull his tail.
d	Her false teeth would have broken	if she had known that I
e	The cat will scratch you	needed it.
f	She would look much better	if you ask him.
g	Aunt Florrie would have lent me	if she had dropped them.
	her car	if they touch that wire.
h	Would you marry me	if you had asked me.
i	The plants would die	if she combed her hair.
j	I would have gone to the dentist's	if we didn't water them.

3 Now, in these conditional sentences, put the verbs into their correct forms.

a You (*spend*) less money if you had gone to the supermarket.

b The policeman (*tell*) you the way if you ask him nicely.

c If it (*rain*) tomorrow, we (*stay*) at home instead of going to the beach.

d If I (*win*) a lot of money in a lottery, I (*go*) to Honolulu for my holiday next year.

e The bell (*ring*) if you (*press*) that button.

f Uncle Jeremiah (*help*) you if he (*have*) time, but he is always very busy.

g If you (*look*) before crossing the road you (*see*) the lorry coming, and you wouldn't be in hospital now.

h I (*come*) next Thursday evening if I (*finish*) work early.

i If she (*wear*) less make-up, she (*be*) very attractive.

4 '*I wear false teeth, dear*' . . . '*So do I*'. (*l.* 51–53) When *so* is used to express agreement with a statement, there is inversion of subject and verb; *do* and *did* are used for ordinary finite verbs in the simple present and past.

Examples: *She wears false teeth and her husband wears false teeth too* would be better expressed as 'She wears false teeth and so does her husband'.

She has been very ill and her husband has been very ill too becomes 'She has been very ill and so has her husband'.

Neither is used in exactly the same way for agreement with negative statements: *She doesn't wear false teeth and neither does her husband.*

Rewrite and improve these sentences in the same way, using *so* or *neither*.

a Mr Crawford works in the City and Mr Bentley works there too.

b Buses are very expensive these days and trains are very expensive too.

c I don't like fish very much and my wife doesn't like fish very much either.

d I was born in Manchester and my wife was born in Manchester.

e Switzerland isn't a very big country, and Belgium and Holland aren't very big countries.

f She won't be at the wedding and her two sisters won't be at the wedding either.

g Aunt Mary lives near the gas-works and Aunt Jane lives near the gas-works.

h Mrs Garland is going to Canada next year and her sixteen children are going too.

i She gave me a kiss when I arrived and her sister kissed me as well.

j Mozart started composing music when he was very young and Schubert started composing music when he was very young as well.

k We have three children and our neighbours have three children too.

l The news wasn't very good on Wednesday and the weather forecast wasn't very good.

m Susan will be at the party and Peter will be at the party and Paul will be at the party.

n The soup wasn't very hot and the main course wasn't very hot.

o Bears usually go to sleep in the winter and many other animals usually go to sleep in the winter.

p Shakespeare wrote a lot of plays and Shaw wrote a lot of plays.

q The hotel near the station is not very good, and the hotel on the other side of the market square is not very good either.

5 Write a letter to Abby, in not more than 150 words. You can either continue with the topic of false teeth, making some observations of your own or giving advice from your personal experience, or you can begin a completely new correspondence and invent a problem of your own. Notice that the letters are all written in a very friendly and informal way; try to write yours in the same style.

6 Tell this story in your own words. Begin: 'When Gaye found a red mark . . .'

Art world mourns Picasso

PABLO PICASSO died yesterday in the South of France, aged 91.

Colleagues in the art world described him as the man who invented
5 modern painting, the greatest painter of the century and among the great painters of all time.

Picasso died of a heart attack in his 35-room country home near the small
10 town of Mougins, after a lingering illness.

Among the mourners in Picasso's mansion, Notre Dame de Vie, were his wife, Jacqueline, 47, and his son,
15 Paolo, 52, only child of his first marriage to Russian dancer Olga Kolkova.

PIONEER

A spokesman for the family said no
20 funeral arrangements had yet been made.

Picasso, pioneer of cubism and most controversial artist of the century, had lived in exile in France
25 since the Spanish Civil War of 1936–39, vowing he would never return to his native Spain until the republic was restored there.

For the lifetime of most people, he
30 had always been painting, and the reaction of many in France and abroad on hearing of his death was one almost of surprise to learn he was not immortal.

35 Italian sculptor Giacomo Manzu, a personal friend of the painter, said in Rome Picasso was 'the man who invented modern painting.'

SYMBOL

A painter and sculptor of prodi- 40 gious talent, he spent virtually the whole of his working life in France.

He was born on October 25th, 1881, at Malaga, son of Jose Ruiz Blasco, an art teacher, and Maria 45 Picasso.

He first went to Paris in 1900 and settled there in 1904. His first years in Paris were those of his 'Blue Period' when blue predominated in 50 his melancholic pictures of sorrowful, hungry people.

In 1907 came a major turning point, when he painted 'Les Demoi-selles d'Avignon'. 55

This was his first step towards cubism, of which he was the pioneer and master.

After the second world war, he made his major political gesture by 60 declaring his allegiance to the Communist Party.

He produced anti-war pictures like 'Korean Massacres' and two great panels 'War and Peace'. 65

He also designed the dove symbol —the famous 'Dove of Peace'—for the Communist-led World Peace Congress in Paris in 1948.

---

lingering (l. 10) lasting a long time

pioneer (l. 18) someone who begins or initiates a movement or style

cubism (l. 22) an art style in which things are represented as geometrical shapes

1 The answer to the question 'Who died on 8th April 1973?' would be *Pablo Picasso*. Using only information from the story, write possible questions to which these phrases could be the answers.

a in the South of France

b a heart attack

c 35

d near Mougins

e 47

f 1936–1939

g Italian

h 1900

i because blue predominated in his pictures

j cubism

Now write similar short answers for these questions:

k How old was Picasso when he died?

l Who was Olga Kolkova?

m What was Olga Kolkova?

n Who is Giacomo Manzu?

o Who was Jose Ruiz Blasco?

p What was Picasso's father?

q What was a major turning point in his career?

r What is 'Korean Massacres'?

s What was the dove symbol?

t What happened in Paris in 1948?

2 Picasso died *of* a heart attack *in* his 35-room country house *near* the small town *of* Mougins, *after* a lingering illness. *Among* the mourners *in* Picasso's mansion . . . (*l.* 8–13)

Now put suitable prepositions or conjunctions in the spaces below.

a There is a strange smell _____ the kitchen. I don't know whether it is coming _____ the big cupboard _____ the wall, or the small one _____ the sink. _____ the other hand, it may be the cheese I bought _____ my visit _____ the mountains _____ the end of last month. I left it _____ a shelf, wrapped _____ _____ a piece of paper, because there was no room _____ the refrigerator.

b After walking _____ about an hour, we reached a little village _____ the top _____ a hill. It was obviously not the place we were looking _____, so we carried _____ walking. A few miles _____ the village, the road divided, and we had no means _____ knowing which of the two ways would lead us _____ our destination, as there was no sign _____ help us. _____ talking it _____ _____ a few minutes, we decided _____ the track that led _____ the hill _____ the stream which we could see glistening _____ the valley.

c Children _____ five years _____ age are not compelled to go _____ school _____ England, but _____ that age education is compulsory. There are primary schools _____ children aged _____ five _____ eleven, and _____ that they go _____ to grammar schools or secondary modern schools. _____ the

bigger towns there are also comprehensive schools; these cater
_____ the needs _____ children who would otherwise go _____
the three other types _____ school.

3 Among the mourners in Picasso's *mansion* . . . (*l.* 12–13). A mansion
is a very large house. Here are nine other types of house. Put each one
into its appropriate sentence.

> bungalow   castle   flat   home   hut   caravan
> cottage   shed   palace

a After our marriage we lived in a two-roomed _____ in South
London.
b There is a little _____ for climbers near the top of the mountain.
c Uncle Gregory has just bought a _____ to pull behind his car.
d Grandmother lives in a _____ because she is too old to go up and
down stairs.
e The _____ was attacked by a large army of enemy soldiers.
f I keep the lawnmower and all my garden tools in a little _____
behind the house.
g Buckingham _____ is the London home of the Queen.
h They live in a picturesque little old _____ on the edge of the forest.
i Let's go _____ ; I'm tired and I want to go to bed.

4 Picasso had lived in France *since* the Civil War. (*l.* 22–25) *For* the
lifetime of most people he had always been painting . . . (*l.* 29–30)

Put *for* or *since* in these sentences

a I haven't heard from her _____ she went abroad.
b We have lived in the same house _____ twenty-five years.
c The shop has been closed _____ last month.
d They have been on holiday at the seaside _____ the last month.
e How many cigarettes have you smoked _____ breakfast?
f Picasso lived in France _____ many years.
g Those old houses have stood there _____ centuries.
h He hasn't visited us _____ we moved to our new house.
i You haven't kissed me _____ ages.
j Aunt Rachel hasn't ridden a bicycle _____ she was a girl.

5 His first years in Paris were those of his 'Blue Period'. (*l.* 48–50)
Colours are often used in an idiomatic sense. Put the appropriate
colours into these sentences.

a John's wife hit him when he came home late last night, and now
he has a _____ eye.
b You must be _____ if you can believe such a silly story!
c 'How are you?' 'I'm fine, thanks. In fact, I'm in the _____.'
d Such strange things happen only once in a _____ moon.

e My sister will be _____ with envy when she sees my beautiful new diamond ring.

f Be careful what you say to Father. He's in a _____ mood this morning.

g Somebody hit me on the head, and everything went _____.

6 This obituary (an article of appreciation written on the death of someone) is about 350 words long. Rewrite it, using not more than 100 words.

7 Write a similar obituary for someone famous in your own country who has died recently. Use about 300 words.

8

Clues across

1 Mozart wrote 'The _____ Flute' and Aladdin had a _____ lamp (5)
4 There are many kinds of this; writing, wrapping and blotting (5)
7 Everything (3)
8 Gramophone records (5)
9 Watchful, vigilant (5)
10 'Make _____ while the sun shines' (3)
12 Female servant (4)
14 'A rolling stone gathers no ____' (4)
15 Pairs (7)
16 A rough, bad-mannered man (4)
17 Where a shopkeeper may keep his money (4)
19 Verb: to wager (3)
21 Verb: to reduce to powder by rubbing on something rough (5)
22 Fruit found round the Mediterranean; its oil is used everywhere (5)
23 'Much _____ about Nothing' (Shakespeare) (3)
24 Verb with three meanings: one is to pay for someone's drink (5)
25 Sometimes the meaning is not quite clear, and then you must read between the _____ (5)

Clues down

1 A polite way of addressing a woman (5)
2 Frenchmen and Italians do it when they speak (11)
3 Money (4)
4 You may see this in the theatre (4)
5 A grammatical term: by, with, to, etc. (11)
6 Tax that British householders pay (5)
11 Common fruit; Eve ate one (5)
13 A spot or point (3)
14 Past tense of meet (3)
16 'Many hands make _____ work' (5)
18 Vegetables: national emblem of Wales (5)
19 Verb with many meanings: one is to conquer (4)
20 A hammer is one; a saw is another (4)

Cinema

by Richard Mallett

WHAT ARE commonly called "horror stories" as a rule leave me cold, but **The Possession of Joel Delaney** (at the Astoria and the Metropole; director, Waris Hussein) is remarkably good and extremely effective. One reason for this is the central player, Shirley MacLaine, whom in any vein it is hard to resist—but we're used to her mostly in comedy parts: she is a superb comedienne. Here she displays her powers as a serious actress, and the result is impressive.

She is Norah Benson, divorced, with two young children, and the spring of the action to begin with is her horrified sight of the arrest of her beloved brother Joel Delaney (Perry King) as he wildly, insanely fights with the police on the steps of his apartment house in the Puerto Rican district of New York. She goes to the police station to make inquiries, and is choked off (all such details are presented with dreadful believability)—and then, when she is at last allowed to visit him, he insists that he had *not* been (as the police assumed) on an LSD trip, and that he remembers absolutely nothing about the occasion anyway. Apparently he attacked the care-taker and tried to murder him, but he has no memory of it, and no motive. Never, he declares, has he taken drugs at all.

The story has too many ramifications to detail, as usual with anything from a novel (by Ramona Stewart; script by Matt Robinson and Grimes Grice), but the point in the end turns out to be that Joel is "possessed" by the spirit of his great friend, a young Puerto Rican, who it seems was killed some months earlier. All this emerges little by little in various ways.

There is a great deal about voodoo and so forth—and what is unusual, what may be for many people unsatisfactory, is that there's no attempt at explanation. We're left to assume that Joel *was* genuinely "possessed" by the spirit of another . . . who had an inconvenient taste for murdering girls by decapitation.

The point, as with all shockers, is suspense; and the scene at the end when Norah has taken the children to the beach house and put them to bed, and then suddenly finds Joel (now utterly "possessed", speaking only Spanish) coming at her with a flick-knife—this is most powerfully effective.

Altogether, though it is in essentials a plain shocker, it's extremely well done. Besides the excellent, convincing incidental detail, I remember particularly some first-rate visual effects (colour photography by **Arthur J. Ornitz**)

she is choked off (l. 27) The police send her away without explaining anything, and pretend that nothing is wrong

to be on an LSD trip (l. 33) to be under the influence of the drug LSD

ramifications (l. 42) complications

1 Read the film review carefully. Then choose the correct answers in the following exercise.

a The writer, Richard Mallett,

  a loves horror films.
  b doesn't usually like horror films.
  c hates horror films.

b Shirley MacLaine, according to the writer,

  a is a better comedienne than a serious actress.
  b usually acts in comedies.
  c is better as a serious actress than as a comedienne.

c The story is very complicated because

  a it is adapted from a novel.
  b it was written by Ramona Stewart.
  c the story emerges little by little.

d Joel Delaney's dead friend was

  a a killer.
  b a spirit.
  c decapitated.

e Mr Mallett's opinion of the film is that it is

  a shocking and plain.
  b colourful and excellent.
  c well-acted and well-made.

2 Correct the following sentences about the film review.

a Mr Richard Mallett doesn't usually like Shirley MacLaine.
b Norah Benson lives in the Puerto Rican district of New York.
c The police arrested Joel Delaney because he was under the influence of LSD.
d The novel, from which the film was made, was written by Matt Robinson and Grimes Grice.
e What for many people may be unsatisfactory about the film is that there is a good deal in it about voodoo.

3 Here she *displays* her powers as a serious actress. (*l.* 13–14) Look at these ten verbs, which have certain similarities in meaning, and at the sentences that follow them. Put each verb (in its appropriate form) into its correct sentence.

> display   reveal   show   exhibit   model
> demonstrate   publish   indicate   disclose
> discover

a Will you please _____ me where I can leave my coat?
b The artist _____ his life story last year.

c The dresses and coats were _____ by two very elegant thin young women.

d We have enlarged our shop windows so that we can _____ more goods.

e I had a terrible shock when I _____ a body under my bed.

f Will you _____ the machine to me, please?

g She _____ the direction with a slight nod of the head.

h My artist cousin _____ his pictures in London, Rome and Berlin.

i The actress _____ in an interview that she had once been married to a policeman.

j They drew back the curtain and _____ a small door.

4 ... the arrest of her beloved brother, Joel Delaney. (*l.* 20–21) In this sentence, *beloved* is an adjective, and must be pronounced as three syllables; *be-lo-ved*. When the word is used in other senses, as a verb or participle, it has only two syllables; *be-lov'd*. Other words, in which the final *-ed* must be pronounced as a separate syllable only when used as adjectives, are *blessed*, *cursed*, *learned*, *aged*. Now, read the following sentences aloud.

a My grandmother has aged considerably since I last saw her.

b The judge is an aged man and very wise.

c The judge is also a very learned man.

d He learned a lot during his stay in India.

e This cursed car still won't start although I have been working on it all morning.

f When her husband sold her jewellery, she lost her temper and cursed him loudly.

g At the end of the service, the priest turned and blessed the people.

h I can't find my blessed keys anywhere.

i Although he was a hardened criminal, he was beloved by his wife and children.

5 ... and then, when she is *at last* allowed to visit him. (*l.* 29–31) Look at these expressions, which have certain similarities in meaning, and the sentences that follow them. Put each expression into its correct sentence.

at last   finally   in the end   eventually   in case

in conclusion   consequently   naturally

in the event of   lately

a Ah! You have arrived _____ ! I have been waiting for three hours.

b If you work really hard, you are sure to pass the examination _____ .

c I haven't been feeling very well _____ .

d And now, ladies and gentlemen, _____ , may I thank you all for listening to me.

e We called at Gibraltar, Malta, Cyprus, and _____ Istanbul.

f She got very wet and _____ caught a cold.

g Take an umbrella with you _____ it rains.

h _____, I am very fond of my two brothers.

i _____ fire, dial '999' and ask for the Fire Brigade.

j We shall have to pay the bill _____, so let's do it at once.

6 . . . who had an inconvenient taste for murdering girls by *decapitation*. (*l*. 60–62) Think for a moment of other ways of murdering than by decapitation. Fill in the missing verbs in these sentences, all of which describe ways of killing.

a He _____ her in the back with a knife.

b She _____ her husband by putting arsenic in his coffee.

c Othello _____ his wife, Desdemona, with a pillow.

d Anne Boleyn was _____ with an axe.

e The poor man _____ himself from a tree in the garden.

f I pushed him off the bridge, and, as he could not swim, he _____.

g She took a pistol out of her handbag and calmly _____ him in the chest.

h Marie Antoinette was _____ in 1793.

i They gave their prisoner no food and finally _____ him to death.

7 . . . suddenly finds Joel (now utterly possessed, speaking only *Spanish*). (*l*. 68–70) Fill in the spaces in the following sentences.

Example: Juan comes from Spain. He is a Spaniard and he speaks Spanish.

a Pierre comes from France.   He is a _____ and he speaks _____.

b Birgit comes from Denmark.   She is a _____ and she speaks _____.

c Zafer comes from Turkey.   He is a _____ and he speaks _____.

d Michael comes from Athens.   He is a _____ and he speaks _____.

e Anita comes from Sweden.   She is a _____ and she speaks _____.

f Hans-Peter comes from Switzerland.   He is a _____ and he speaks _____.

g Jens comes from Iceland.   He is an _____ and he speaks _____.

h Olga comes from Russia.   She is a _____ and she speaks _____.

i Shuhei comes from Japan.   He is a _____ and he speaks _____.

j Iris comes from Finland.   She is a _____ and she speaks _____.

8 The film review of 'The Possession of Joel Delaney' is slightly over 400 words long. Imagine that you are the editor of the magazine, and you have to reduce this article to not more than 150 words. Don't forget that you must give your readers the same information and impression of the film as they would get from the longer article.

9 Write a review, in a similar style of any film you have seen recently. You can recommend your readers to go to see it, or you can advise them that it is not worth seeing, but, in either case, you must give reasons for your judgement. You should also give enough details of the story to make them interested. Use about 300 words.

26

THE GUARDIAN
September 29, 1972

Doctor's home cure

By our own Reporter

A COUNTRY doctor in Milton-under-Wychwood, Oxfordshire, has offered a £5,000 interest-free loan to help young couples in the area to form a housing society.

Dr Gordon Scott, aged 66, who lives in the Cotswolds village has put up the money because young people are unable to afford the high price of local property.

"Many of the small cottages around the village have been bought as weekend retreats by the wealthy and I think it is pathetic that the young should have to leave the villages where they were born. New houses are far beyond the pockets of young couples."

Originally Dr Scott wanted to form a housing society which would buy cottages. But as a result of a meeting which he called he said it now seemed best to form a society to buy land and build houses. Members would build their own homes.

Dr Scott, who retires tomorrow, has lived in the village for nine years. He has been a family doctor in the Cotswolds for 36 years. He paid £5,500 for his own house and more recently made "a nice profit" from selling off building land.

"I don't see why I should not share it around a bit. I cannot take it with me when I go." His contribution will go towards initial costs of legal fees, fighting for planning permission and, hopefully, laying out a road system.

Reaction to his plan from young people had been very good, said Dr Scott, but he understood there was disapproval in some quarters about the prospect of more building in the village. "Ironically, it seems to be coming from the people who have moved into the village comparatively recently."

I cannot take it with me when I go (l. 41–43)
I cannot take my money with me when I die

1 *Dr Scott has offered a £5,000 interest-free loan.* (*l.* 3–4)

An *interest-free* loan is a loan that is free of interest. Use similar compound adjectives to express the following ideas.

Example: A swimming pool in the open air = *an open-air swimming pool.*

a a tiger that eats men
b a job that consumes a lot of time
c a flower that smells sweet
d an event that has been forgotten for a long time
e a suit made by a tailor
f a plane that flies high
g a garden that nobody cares for
h goods that are free of tax
i an atmosphere which is free of germs
j a beetle that bores into wood

Now, what do you understand by the following expressions?

k a six-sided coin
l a double-decker bus
m a nearly-forgotten face
n a six-storeyed building
o a quickly-done job

p an eye-opening remark
q a long-awaited decision
r a half-expected development
s a generally-accepted plan
t a mouth-watering dish

2 Dr Scott has *put up* the money because young people are unable to afford the high price of local property. (*l.* 7–12)

Fill in the spaces in the following sentences, all of which use *put* in various ways.

a I have put _____ _____ a transfer to the Birmingham division.
b Uncle Victor was very put _____ to find that his wife had run away with the milkman.
c I can't put _____ _____ that noise any longer! For Heaven's sake, stop it!
d Mrs Bragsby-Prout was shocked when the rude little girl put her tongue _____ _____ her.
e He managed to put _____ a quarter of his salary every month.
f Not only are his ideas sound, but he manages to put them _____ to his students very well.
g Put _____ that book and listen to me!
h Don't think about it any more; put it _____ of your mind.
i Poor thing! After her husband died, she went quite mad and had to be put _____.
j Never put _____ until tomorrow what you can do today.

3 *Milton-under-Wychwood* is the answer to the question 'Where does Dr Scott live?'. Write questions to which these phrases might be the answers (using only information from the story).

a Oxfordshire
b to form a housing society
c because prices of property are so high
d because they have been bought as weekend retreats by the wealthy
e after a meeting
f tomorrow
g nine years
h 36 years
i selling land for building
j people who have only recently moved to the village

4 Many of the small cottages around the village have been bought by *the wealthy* and I think it is pathetic that *the young* should have to leave the villages where they were born. (*l.* 13–19)

The + an adjective is a general term; *the wealthy* means 'wealthy people in general'; *the young* means 'young people in general'.

Rewrite these sentences, using this construction in place of the phrases in *italics*.

a *People who are sick* are cared for in hospitals or nursing homes.
b After the accident *the injured people* were taken away in an ambulance.
c The news will be of great interest to *people who have got married recently*.
d We are collecting money to give an outing to *all the people in the village who are poor*.
e White sticks are usually carried by *people who are blind*.
f The exam is so easy that only *people who are very stupid* could fail to pass it.
g *People who feel nervous* should sleep with their windows closed.
h Do you think that *people who are colour blind* should be permitted to drive?
i Modern electronic devices have made it much easier for *people who are deaf* to lead a normal life.
j *People who have fair skins* should not stay in the sun for too long.

5 *Ironically*, it seems to be coming from the people who have moved into the village *comparatively* recently. (*l.* 56–59)

In words of more than two syllables, it is sometimes difficult to know which syllable should be accented. In this sentence, the two examples are ir*on*ically and com*par*atively.

Underline the accented syllable in these words.

irony   ironical   photograph   photographer
photographic   benefit   beneficial   medicine
medical   medicinal   medicate   sympathy
sympathetic   probable   probability   illuminate
illumination   compete   competition   competitive

6 Imagine that you are one of the young people in Milton-under-Wychwood who will be able to benefit from Dr Scott's loan. Write the story in your own words (only information contained in the passage should be used) of Dr Scott's decision.

7 What are the particular housing problems in your own area? What do you think should be done to provide houses for young people? Write your own ideas on the subject in about 250 words.

8

Clues across

5 Adjective: a hill may be this; so may stairs, and prices too (5)
6 Flower from which opium comes (5)
8 Childish word for Mother (2)
9 The doctor may give you these to swallow (5)
10 Third person singular of the verb to be (2)
12 Everything (3)
14 Influenza (3)
15 A pleasant place for a holiday (7)
16 Romeo _____ Juliet (3)
18 Organ of sight (3)
20 Pronoun (2)
21 If you cut yourself, you will _____ (5)
23 On the other hand; otherwise (2)
24 Try not to meet (5)
25 A porter's job is to _____ luggage (5)

Clues down

1 Rob (5)
2 Verb: to have a quick look (4)
3 Verb: what an angry bull may do if he catches you (4)
4 Verb: to ruin (5)
7 You may get one on your foot if your shoes are too tight (7)
8 Feminine of sir (5)
11 'Man and _____ man' (Shaw) (5)
13 A drug (3)
14 The money you pay for professional services (3)
17 If the dentist drills on it, you will shout! (5)
19 Not mine (5)
21 Edge (4)
22 Part of the telephone, with letters and figures (4)

27

DAILY AMERICAN
January 18, 1972

Blacksmith laments absence of horses

NAPOLEON, Ohio, Jan. 18. (AP) - Matt Becker is a wiry 84 - year - old man who knows he is
5 one of a dying breed.

He's a blacksmith, a trade he has followed 66 years and still works at six - days a week.
10 He came to the United States from Germany when he was 18, after learning the blacksmith trade from his
15 grandfather.

"I didn't like it at first because I couldn't speak English," Becker said of the trade in his new
20 country. But he stuck with it because "it's the only thing I know."

He walks one mile each morning from his home to
25 the rustic old shop, considered a local landmark. "I want to work as long as I'm able," he said.
30 The thing he misses most from his work in a modern world is horses. "I haven't shod a horse in 30 years," he said.
35 "Shoeing horses started slacking off around 1940. Besides, I couldn't handle one at my age anyway."

Although he still uses
40 many of the old tools of his trade, most of his work now is spent

Matt Becker, 84, works in his blacksmith shop at Napoleon, Ohio, where he has been a blacksmith since 1920. Becker learned the trade 66 years ago in his native Germany.

sharpening blades for mowers and repairing parts for tractors and 45 farm implements.

He said many farmers in the area come to him "because I can fix things for them that might take 50 weeks to have repaired at a factory."

Motorists passing his shop often hear the clang of hammer on metal as he 55 shapes a piece of metal on his anvil.

He started his shop here in 1920 as a partnership but soon 60 bought out his partner because there was not enough work for two men.

"When I'm gone," he noted, "there won't be a 65 blacksmith in this town."

wiry (l. 3) thin, but very strong and muscular

to shoe (l. 33) to fit iron shoes to horses. (Irregular verb: shoe – shod – shod)

anvil (l. 57) a large block of iron on which the blacksmith works his hot metal

1 **a** He knows he is one of a dying breed (*l.* 4–5) means

   a he knows there are not many blacksmiths working now.
   b he knows that he is very old and he is going to die soon.
   c he knows that he is one of the last members of the Becker family.

b He stuck with it (*l.* 20–21) means

   a he didn't give up.
   b he was forced to do it.
   c he got very bored with it.

c Considered a local landmark (*l.* 26–27) means

   a thought to be very beautiful.
   b of great historical interest.
   c very well-known and conspicuous.

d I want to work as long as I'm able (*l.* 27–29) means

   a I want to work very long hours every day when I can.
   b I want to work until it isn't possible for me to work any more.
   c I want to keep the shop open very late in the evening.

e Shoeing horses started slacking off around 1940 (*l.* 35–36) means

   a after 1940 he was paid less for shoeing each horse.
   b horses have not been very well shod since 1940.
   c there were fewer and fewer horses to be shod after 1940.

2 He's a blacksmith, a *trade* he has followed for 66 years. (*l.* 6–8)

Look at these ten words, which have certain similarities in meaning, and at the ten sentences that follow them. Put each word into its appropriate sentence.

> trade   job   business   profession   vocation
> practice   living   craft   industry   commerce

a He qualified as a dentist in 1969, and set up in _____ in Sheffield.
b After leaving school, I got a _____ in a solicitor's office.
c I would like my son to take over the _____ when I retire.
d Nursing is not just a job; it is a _____, calling for much self-sacrifice and devotion.
e She earns her _____ by telling fortunes at the seaside.
f The ancient _____ of weaving has been carried on in these islands for centuries.
g My Uncle Joshua has worked in the local Chamber of _____ since he graduated from Oxford.
h Our _____ mark is a circle with the letters 'G L' inside it.
i There are a lot of Scotsmen in the medical _____.
j It's a dirty, smoky city, as there is a lot of heavy _____ on the outskirts.

3 'I haven't shod a horse *in* 30 years,' he said. (*l.* 33–34) This is an Americanism, not used in other parts of the English-speaking world. The more usual forms are *for* and *since*. 'I haven't shod a horse *for* 30 years.' or 'I haven't shod a horse *since* 1942'.

Put *for* or *since* in these sentences.

a He has worked as a blacksmith _____ he was a boy.
b It has been raining _____ ten o'clock; I hope it will stop soon.
c He has been a blacksmith _____ 66 years.
d I still haven't found a rich wife although I have been looking for one ever _____ I was 20.
e She has lived a very quiet life _____ her husband died.
f The water has been boiling _____ four minutes, so the egg should be cooked by now.
g We enjoyed the film very much, even though we had to wait _____ half an hour to get into the cinema.
h He lived in Germany _____ the first 18 years of his life.
i There has been a lighthouse on that rock _____ at least four hundred years.
j Cousin Araminta has been in hospital _____ the middle of January.

4 He started his shop here in 1920 as a partnership *but* soon bought out his partner *because* there was not enough work for two men. (*l.* 58–63) Here, three short sentences have been joined together with *but* and *because*. Join these sentences together, using the words suggested.

a Angela is one of my best friends. She did not invite me to her party. (*although*)
b I was having a picnic. I sat on a wasp. I got up very quickly. (*while, so*)
c The people threw rotten tomatoes. The Prime Minister arrived. (*when*)
d They were late. They made a lot of noise. (*not only . . . but . . . as well*)
e He sings very well. He plays the flute very well. (*both . . . and*)
f I came back from my holiday in Hawaii. I was very sun-tanned. (*when*)
g You can come on Monday. You can come on Thursday. (*either . . . or*)
h She can't act. She has a beautiful figure. She has been given the leading part in a new film. (*although, so*)

5 The headline for this news story is BLACKSMITH LAMENTS ABSENCE OF HORSES. A good headline should sum up, in as few words as possible, the main points of interest of the story. Read the following short news items. Imagine that you are the news editor, and write suitable headlines for them. Each headline should be of no more than four words.

a 65-year-old Mrs Gladys Crump, mother of five and grandmother of eight, won first prize yesterday in a driving competition organized by the local branch of the Auto Club. Mrs Crump, who said, 'This is the first time in my life that I have ever won anything,' plans to spend the £200 on a seaside holiday with her husband.

b The Managing Director of the Achilles Motor Company, 38-year-old Mr Desmond Druce, told the Annual General Meeting yesterday that during the past twelve months more Achilles cars had been sold than in any other year since the foundation of the company, nearly twenty years ago.

c Sir Caleb Smithers, who was Minister of Supply in the years immediately following the Second World War, left £545,723 in his will published yesterday. Sir Caleb, who was a well-known bridge-player and patron of the arts, died at his home in Wales on March 4th last year, aged 93.

d Police were called in to control the crowds of angry teenagers outside Verrybridge Stadium last night. More than seven thousand youngsters had been unable to get in to hear 'The Falling Rocks', whose concert had been fully booked since the first day it was announced, three months ago. Mr Alec Gough, 'The Falling Rocks' manager, said that he hoped to arrange for the group to give another concert in the area very soon.

6 Now, write similar short news items (like those in question 5) of about the same length which might be found under the following headlines. Invent any facts you think are necessary.

a MOTHER FINED FOR SHOP-LIFTING
b WORLD TOUR FOR PIANIST
c LAWYER JAILED FOR THEFT
d ROVERS LOSE TWO NIL
e POSTAL STRIKE CALLED OFF

7 There are about 270 words in the story about Matt Becker. Rewrite it for a second edition of the newspaper, using not more than 100 words.

8 Tell the story in your own words. Begin: Before George and Gaye went on holiday . . .

28

THE SUNDAY TIMES
May 6, 1973

Barbara Cartland, author-ess and naturalist, has just completed a book, to be published in O c t o b e r,
5 **about men and their passion for sport. It seemed an excellent time for ROB HUGHES to ask her about women in sport.**

10 ● *What do you think of the willingness of many women to become sports widows*

Women are silly asses if they become sports widows. If you've
15 got a husband who's a terrific football fan, the sooner you learn about football the better. A woman's job in life is to inspire the men. It's like the theatre,
20 you don't have to act to enjoy what's going on. ℓ

●*Do you still take part in any sports?*

Oh dear! I don't actually wave
25 my legs around my head if that's what you mean, because I simply haven't time. If you live with men as I've always done, because I have two brothers as well as two sons, you soon find that no-
30 body actually *wants* a woman to show off. They want to show off to you. I've watched, and said "wonderful, wonderful."

● *What sports have you tried?* 35

I played tennis, rather feebly; I used to swim, badly, but I must admit I do *fish* rather well —salmon fishing. My daughter (Lady Dartmouth) has been
40 terribly athletic and my mother, who's now 95, played cricket. She was a very good bowler, but I think women look absolute fools playing cricket and football.
45 Women's *real* sport is chasing men.

● *Mary Peters, our only gold athletics winner at the last Olympics, won an endurance*
50 *event. Presumably you wouldn't consider that very feminine*

No, I don't think it *is* very feminine, although I do think it's splendid if anyone of our people
55 can do that. We treat sports-people terribly. We've got *millions* of absolutely excellent athletes in this country, but they work very hard, nine to six, for
60 five days a week and they eat fish and chips.

sports widows (l. 12) women whose husbands are never at home because they are too busy with sport

a terrific football fan (l. 15–16) a person who is very fond of football

1 *October* might be the answer to the question: 'When is Barbara Cartland's book to be published?'.

Here are eight 'answers'. Using the information in the passage, write the questions that they answer.

a men and their passion for   e chasing men
    sport   f Mary Peters
b to inspire the men   g terribly
c I simply haven't time   h very hard
d they want to show off to you

2 *The sooner you learn about football the better.* (*l.* 16–17) This is another way of saying that the best thing to do is to learn about football at the first opportunity. Notice the construction – *the sooner . . . the better.* Here is another example: *The more food you eat the fatter you will become.*

Rewrite these sentences, using this construction, to give the same idea. You may have to change the words considerably.

a You are already wet, and if you stand here in the rain any longer you will get even wetter.

b He grew very angry when we laughed, so we laughed more and he was even angrier.

c Antique chairs cost a lot of money, and older ones are even more expensive.

d My brother likes doing crossword puzzles, and he likes them to be as difficult as possible.

e As I get older I become more contented.

f Your cough is bad and if you smoke more it will be worse.

g Big trees give a lot of shade, and bigger trees give even more shade.

h Clothes wear out, and cheaper clothes wear out even more quickly.

3 This piece is all about sport. Fill in the spaces in the following sentences with suitable words.

a There was a big crowd at Eastwood Stadium last night to see the football _____ between Ayton Wanderers and Beaton United. The two _____ played very well, but United managed to win by two _____ to one. When the final _____ blew, the crowd rushed onto the _____ to congratulate the _____ .

b Miss Cartland says that she is good at fishing. For this sport you need a lot of patience, especially if you have to sit on the river bank for hours, watching the _____ bobbing about in the water, without getting a _____ . You must also be very careful when you put the _____ on the _____ , or you may injure your fingers badly. When a fish has taken the _____ , you can feel a pull on the end of your _____ , and this is the most exciting moment of all.

c I put the rifle to my shoulder and took _____, closing my left eye, and looking through the sight at the _____. I could see the rings of red and black quite clearly. Gently, I pulled the _____ and I felt the shock on my shoulder and on my cheek as the gun _____. I took a _____ from the little box beside me and _____ the gun again. I _____ six shots altogether, and I was very pleased to see, later, that there were six little round holes right in the centre of the _____.

d We went to the tennis _____ before breakfast, when there was nobody there. Both Martin and I wanted to practise before the important _____ later in the morning. I was very pleased with the new _____ I had bought the day before, which was not quite as heavy as the one I had played with previously. Martin _____ to me from the other end, but the first _____ hit the _____. The second one came over, and I returned it quite gently, but Martin was not able to reach it before it _____ a second time, so the first _____ was mine. Martin won the second, making the _____ fifteen-all.

4 *I used to swim.* (*l.* 37) Fill in the spaces in the following sentences, using suitable verbs and the *used to* construction.

a I don't go in for sport now, but I _____ football when I was younger.

b They _____ in Bradford but now they have a flat in Leeds.

c I _____ French quite well, but I'm afraid I've forgotten most of it now.

d When we were children, we always _____ our holidays at the seaside.

e 'Are you fond of winter sports?'
'Well, I _____ when the ice was thick enough, but I haven't done so for many years.'

f They _____ very friendly; I can't think why they don't speak to us now.

g I _____ English food, but I think it is quite pleasant now.

h Yes, Aunt Polly is very ugly now, but she _____ attractive when she was a girl.

5 *Barbara Cartland is an authoress and naturalist. Barbara Cartland has just completed a book.* These two sentences can be joined in two ways.
'Barbara Cartland, authoress and naturalist, has just completed a book.' (*l.* 1–3)
'Barbara Cartland, who has just completed a book, is an authoress and naturalist.'

Join these pairs of sentences in the same way, making two sentences for each pair.

a Katie Green is getting married next Saturday. Katie Green is my best friend.

b Gladstone was one of England's most famous statesmen. Gladstone died in 1898.

c My brother is a very good athlete. My brother lives in York.

d Henry VIII was king of England from 1491 to 1547. Henry VIII had six wives.

e Bob Davy has just got engaged. Bob Davy was last year's 'footballer-of-the-year'.

6 Write an account, in about 300 words, of your favourite sport *or* say what you think about sports for women.

7

Clues across

1 'The Old Man and the _____,' (Hemingway) (3)

5 To _____ fro (3)

6 Pleased, satisfied (7)

7 Definite article (3)

8 Perhaps the last word in the book! (3)

10 Use it after you have washed your hands (5)

13 When a door is _____, it is not completely shut (4)

15 Monkeys (4)

17 Spare time, when you can please yourself what you do (7)

18 A small insect: you would not be pleased to find one! (4)

19 Festival (4)

20 Plural of this (5)

23 A kind of hat (3)

25 Verb: to put plants in the ground (3)

26 Verb: to organise (7)

27 One way of cooking: eggs, for example (3)

28 Question word that asks the reason (3)

Clues down

2 The best card in the pack (3)

3 Preposition indicating movement (4)

4 You come to this place (4)

5 Past tense of eat (3)

7 You see this everywhere at every time, but particularly between 8 and 9 a.m., and 4.30 and 6.30 p.m. (7)

9 Opposite of near (7)

10 Your doctor will _____ you, and perhaps your friends will _____ you too, on your birthday! (5)

11 Verb: to spend time or money, uselessly or foolishly (5)

12 Huge, great, enormous, wide (5)

14 Beer (3)

16 A green vegetable (3)

21 Injured (4)

22 Verb: to make music, in the easiest possible way! (4)

24 You may receive it at the end of the week, or at the end of the month (3)

25 Verb: some women are very good at it, and mothers with young children must do it (3)

29

The Migrant Life

GOSHEN, N.Y. (NYT).—A light bulb hanging from the ceiling illuminates the kitchen in the gray predawn light as Lupe Ortiz starts her day, cooking breakfast for her husband and their nine children. One of about 2,000 migrant workers in Orange County, New York, she is the hardest working member of a hardworking family.

Shaking off her exhaustion, the 39-year-old woman tugs on a woolen workshirt until it stretches across her back and protects her from the damp cold that pervades the cinderblock unit that serves as the family's summer place. The Ortizes are paying off their own home back in Weslaco, Texas, but with no summer work there they come north each year as seasonal agricultural workers.

They are among thousands of other families from the Rio Grande Valley who fan out across the nation each season, like their parents and grandparents before them. It is an exhausting life, a sunup to sundown existence with little time for reflection, even less for fun.

"I don't like moving around," said Mrs. Ortiz, her broad face creased beyond its years from seasons in the fields. "The only thing I like about it here is that we can work."

The summer is a no-nonsense time for Mexican-Americans such as the Ortizes. They come to make money—as much as they can during the harvest—and welcome a long work week. (They make $1.75 an hour at the Sleepy Hollow Growers, Inc., farms in Goshen, a 90-minute drive northwest of New York City. State and federal laws do not provide agricultural workers with such benefits as increased pay for overtime, so they make straight pay even when the week stretches to 70 or 80 hours. A day off provides needed rest but it also deflates the pay envelopes.)

Mrs. Ortiz finishes cooking the bacon and eggs and starts on the lunches she and her husband, Victor, 44, will eat later that day at the packing house.

Normally their two oldest daughters work with them but it is a Sunday and the crops are poor so only one 14-person crew is needed.

The Ortizes live in a unit provided free by Sleepy Hollow that by migrant standards is almost luxurious. "It's so much better than the place we stayed before," Mrs. Ortiz said. "We didn't have any room and it was not clean."

The unit is barren, the only decorations being cardboard pictures of Jesus Christ, the Last Supper and a card congratulating Celia on her graduation from high school. The clothes hang from nails in the wall. The beds double as sofas.

Mrs. Ortiz's daughters sweep the floor and dress the younger children as their mother prepares for work. At 7 a.m., she and Victor are on the ancient bus that takes them and the other workers to the packing house that is processing radishes.

The couple never part. "We always work together, it doesn't matter what crop," Lupe said. This year they have labored side by side weeding and cutting lettuce and celery. Today Lupe will be a sorter, checking radishes for size and blemishes, and Victor will be assembling boxes.

Mrs. Ortiz prefers the packing house to the fields. "At least you don't get so dirty, but it's hard work anyway."

cinderblock unit (l. 14) a building made of a kind of concrete

paying off (l. 16) buying by instalments, so much every month

radishes (l. 71) small, red root vegetables, used in salad

1 Read the story carefully. Then choose the correct answers in the following exercise.

a Families from the Rio Grande Valley

    a have always left home in the summer to look for work elsewhere.
    b have a miserable life with no time for any fun.
    c all go to New York State to work in the summer.

b During the summer, the Ortiz family

    a work for 70–80 hours a week.
    b work as much as they possibly can.
    c take a day off each week.

c The accommodation that the Ortizes are living in is

    a luxurious.
    b not very clean.
    c adequate.

d Lupe and Victor Ortiz have nine children;

    a all the family usually work.
    b four members of the family usually work.
    c none of the children work because they are all at school.

e Mr and Mrs Ortiz

    a always do exactly the same kind of work.
    b never leave the fields.
    c prefer to work together.

2 Lupe Ortiz starts her day, *cooking* breakfast for her husband and their nine children. (*l.* 4–6) Look at the different verbs of cooking listed below, and at the explanations beside them. Find the right explanation that explains each verb of cooking.

Boil	under, or in front of, heat (usually for bread)
Bake	over boiling water
Roast	in boiling water
Fry	slowly in a closed pan or pot
Grill	in the oven (usually for bread or cakes)
Stew	in water, at just below boiling point
Toast	in hot fat or oil
Simmer	under, or in front of, heat (usually for meat)
Steam	in the oven (usually for meat)

3 Shaking *off* her exhaustion, the 39-year-old woman tugs *on* a woollen workshirt until it stretches *across* her back and protects her *from* the damp cold that pervades the cinderblock unit that serves *as* the family's summer place. (*l.* 10–15) The words in *italics* are prepositions. Fill in the correct prepositions in these sentences.

a She poured the beer _____ _____ the jug _____ the glass, but she did it too quickly and the beer ran _____ _____ the table. Now there is a stain _____ the tablecloth, but luckily the liquid did not soak _____ and damage the polished surface _____ the table.

b I must examine you, so take _____ your clothes and lie _____ _____ that couch _____ there. Let me put my stethoscope _____ your chest so that I can listen _____ your heart.

c The man sitting _____ me looked _____ me and winked _____ me. This made me very angry as I had never seen him before _____ my life, so I called _____ my bill and went _____ _____ the cafe as soon as I could.

d We often go _____ _____ Sunday evenings, usually _____ the cinema, but Grandpa always stays _____ home, sitting _____ his big armchair _____ _____ _____ the fire.

e I usually go _____ work _____ bus or train, but this week I am going _____ foot, as all the public transport workers have come _____ _____ strike.

4 This year they have laboured *side by side* weeding and cutting lettuce and celery. (*l.* 74–76) Use the following similar phrases to fill the spaces in these sentences.

> face to face   arm in arm   hand in hand
> hand to hand   hand to mouth   back to back
> heart to heart   nose to tail   tooth and nail
> eye to eye

a Come in and sit down. I want to have a _____ talk with you.

b The main offensive was over, but there was still a lot of _____ fighting going on in the streets.

c The two little boys stood _____ so that their mother could see which was the taller.

d Two old ladies walked down the street _____, both talking at the same time.

e If I ever meet that wicked man _____, I shall tell him exactly what I think of him.

f Mad with anger, the two women fought _____ until the on-lookers managed to part them.

g The two tiny children made a charming picture, wandering through the forest _____.

h I don't get on very well with my uncle; we don't see _____ on many subjects.

i He lived a _____ existence for many years until his artistic genius was finally recognised.

j The roads were crowded with holiday traffic, and cars stretched _____ as far as the eye could see.

5 In not more than 100 words, describe what Lupe Ortiz does from the moment she gets up until she leaves for work.

6 Write a similar account, in the first person this time, of how you spend the same part of your day.

7 Tell the story in your own words. Begin: George and Gaye Gambol went abroad for their summer holiday last year . . .

30

PUNCH
March 14, 1973

There's nothing small about Ontario. No matter where you go in the province you'll experience a sense of unlimited freedom and room to enjoy
5 life. Yet despite more than a quarter million lakes and thousands of square miles of forest rich in fish and game, you are never far from the excitement of big city life.

10 And few cities are as exciting as Ontario's capital, Toronto, Canada's second largest city. It's got the British Commonwealth's largest hotel, the world's largest annual exhibition, the country's longest subway, the largest museum, the busiest stock
15 exchange, the biggest university, and one of the world's most elegant racetracks.

Yet this bustling metropolitan area boasts no fewer than 200 parks. And has transformed Ontario's islands within the city into a magnificent playground,
20 with swimming, sunbathing, tennis, yachting and a

children's farm, only 20 minutes away by ferry. Near-by Black Creek Pioneer Village recreates the colourful development of a typical farm community from 1790–1860.

25 There's Yorkville, with sidewalk cafes, coffee bars and nightly folk entertainment. And you'll want to see Toronto's award-winning City Hall, built in 1965. It's like no other modern
30 government building anywhere in the world.

Toronto is also a centre of road, rail, and air transport, so you can get to virtually anywhere in Canada from here. Even breathtaking Niagara Falls is less than two hours away by coach along the
35 Queen Elizabeth Highway. You'll marvel at this natural splendour – 186 feet tall and 3600 feet wide, it thunders four billion gallons of water an hour over the Horseshoe Falls. You can ride the legendary Maid of the Mist right to the centre of it all, and
40 have a meal 500 feet up in the Skylon Tower.

And as the Falls are the mid-point of a 35 mile system of gardens, parks, and historic sites, there's always plenty to do. A day's coach trip from Toronto to Niagara Falls costs as little as
£4.50 return.
45

For more information about Toronto and other exciting holiday spots in Canada, send this coupon or see your travel agent.

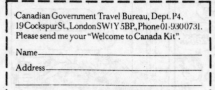

Canadian Government Travel Bureau, Dept. P4,
19 Cockspur St., London SW1Y 5BP, Phone 01-930 0731.
Please send me your "Welcome to Canada Kit".

Name —————————————————

Address —————————————————

————————————————————

Canada

1 Read the advertisement carefully, then give *short* answers to the following questions.

  a What is Ontario?
  b How many lakes are there in Ontario?
  c What can be found in the forests of Ontario?
  d What is Toronto?
  e Where is the biggest university in Canada?
  f Where is Black Creek Pioneer Village?
  g What is special about Toronto's City Hall?
  h How can you go from Toronto to Niagara Falls?
  i How long does the journey take?
  j How much does it cost to go from Toronto to Niagara Falls and back?

2 *200* is the answer to the question 'How many parks are there in Toronto?'. (*l.* 17–18)

Write questions to which these phrases are possible answers.

  a in Toronto
  b no, the second largest
  c Yorkville
  d because it is a centre of road, rail and air transport
  e 186 feet
  f 4 billion gallons
  g a restaurant
  h Cockspur Street
  i by coach
  j by sending the coupon

3 *Few cities are as exciting as Toronto.* (*l.* 10–11) This is another way of saying 'There are not many cities more exciting than Toronto'.

The following ten sentences are written in these two forms. Change each one into the other form.

  a There are not many dramatists more interesting than Shakespeare.
  b Few singers have become as well-known as Frank Sinatra.
  c Few mountains are more difficult to climb than the Eiger.
  d There are not many buildings taller than the United Nations Building.
  e There are not many men richer than Uncle Silas.
  f Few cities have grown more rapidly than Sâo Paolo.
  g Few newspapers are as widely read as the *Daily Express*.
  h There are not many restaurants better than the one in King Street.
  i Few people really understand what happens during a parliamentary debate.
  j There are not many villages that are more difficult to find than Little Twittering.

4 *It's got the British Commonwealth's largest hotel . . . (l. 11–12)*

These sentences are not wrong, but they would sound more natural with the use of the word *got*. Put in the word *got* wherever suitable.

a Mary has to stay at home today because her mother has a new baby and needs some help with the other children.

b 'Have you a ticket?' 'No, I haven't. Why? Have I to have one?' 'Yes. You have to have a valid ticket. As you haven't one, I'm afraid I have to ask you to get off.'

c They have two cars and a couple of servants. You have to admit that he has done very well in recent years.

d Sheila and Ben married when they were very young. They hadn't much money, but they both had very definite ideas about what sort of home they wanted.

e I have an impression that I have something to do this morning, but I haven't the faintest idea what it is. I have a very bad memory.

5 *Even breathtaking Niagara Falls is less than two hours away by coach.* (l. 33–34) 'Niagara Falls – so beautiful that it takes your breath away' can be expressed as *breathtaking Niagara Falls*.

Write similar phrases for these ideas.

a A scream – so loud as to split your ears.
b A sigh – so pitiful as to rend your heart.
c Angela Prendergast's hat – so unusual that it catches your eye.
d Mrs Henderson's cakes – so delicious that they make your mouth water.
e An experience – so frightening as to raise your hair.
f A job – so hard as to break your back.
g Laughter – so hearty as to split your sides.
h A sight – so tragic as to break your heart.
i A story – so frightening as to chill your blood.

6 *It's got the British Commonwealth's largest hotel, the country's longest subway . . . (l. 11–14)*

A large hotel – the largest hotel.
A long subway – the longest subway.

Rewrite these phrases in the same way.

a	a silly person	**i**	a pretty face
b	a beautiful woman	**j**	a religious group
c	a good film	**k**	a torn shirt
d	a sad little girl	**l**	a used room
e	a straight road	**m**	a little-known poet
f	a hated enemy	**n**	a red face
g	an intelligent article	**o**	a badly-written letter
h	a long nose	**p**	a bad mistake

7 The advertisement has been written in such a way as to persuade people to visit Ontario. Write a similar advertisement for your own country or town in about 200 words.

8

Clues across

1 Children like to build them on the beach (4–7)
7 Laid by birds; and eaten by man (3)
8 Vegetable; only one would not make a very good meal! (3)
9 Noise made by a pig – and sometimes by bad-tempered people (5)
11 When you apologise, you say that you are _____ (5)
12 Plural of that (5)
13 A special demonstration, something dangerous, or perhaps an advertising scheme (5)
15 Rivers sometimes do this in a dry season (3-2)
16 Not here (5)
17 'You should _____ to live, and not live to _____' (3)
19 What you expect to have at a party (3)
20 There are hundreds of these in Oxford Street (4–7)

Clues down

1 Cinderella had two of these, and they were very unkind to her (4–7)
2 What a wife may sometimes do to her husband! (3)
3 If something is portable, it means that you can _____ it (5)
4 Verb: to incline, not to be level or straight (5)
5 You have two; an upper one and a lower one (3)
6 Mythical monsters of the ocean (3–8)
9 Verb: to give, to allow (5)
10 You may say this word twice to comfort someone (5)
14 'People who live in glass-houses should not _____ stones' (5)
15 When it rains, the water in the street runs down the _____ (5)
18 It sounds like two and also like to (3)
19 The pendulum of the clock swings to and _____ (3)

LONGMAN GROUP LIMITED
Longman House
Burnt Mill, Harlow, Essex.

©Longman Group Ltd. 1975

All rights reserved. No part of this
publication may be reproduced, stored
in a retrieval system, or transmitted
in any form or by any means, electronic,
mechanical, photocopying, recording, or
otherwise, without the prior permission
of the Copyright owner.

First published 1975
New impressions *1976; *1977 (twice);
*1978; *1979; *1980; *1982

ISBN 0 582 55520 5

Filmset by Keyspools Ltd, Golborne, Lancs.

Printed in Hong Kong by
Commonwealth Printing Press Ltd